THE GEORGIA GUIDESTONES

America's Most Mysterious Monument

Raymond Wiley AND KT Prime

disinformation®
www.disinfo.com

Published by The Disinformation Company Ltd.
111 East 14th Street, Suite 108
New York, NY 10003
www.disinfo.com
books@disinfo.com

Library of Congress Control Number: 2011940512

Designed by Greg Stadnyk

ISBN: 978-1934708-68-2
eISBN: 978-1934708-73-6

Printed in USA

10 9 8 7 6 5 4 3 2 1

Distributed by:
Consortium Book Sales and Distribution
Toll Free: +1.800.283.3572
Fax: +1.800.351.5073
www.cbsd.com

ACKNOWLEDGMENTS

The authors would like to thank the following people for their invaluable assistance in writing this little book: John Robertson, Laura Polmear and Hudson Cone for the photography; Noel Brown for access to his interview with Wyatt Martin; Randall Carlson and Tom Robinson for their informative interviews; Gary, Greg, Amanda and Ralph at Disinformation for all the help with layout, promotions, and the cover; Anita and Laura from Facebook for their help with our research into the Society of the Third Millennium; Graham Hancock and Santha Faiia for their encouragement; the kind people of Elberton, especially Gary Jones at *The Elberton Star*, for all their help and insight; and all the friends and family who supported us over the past year.

TABLE OF CONTENTS

1. The Guidestones

FOREWORD
BY GRAHAM HANCOCK

Not all ancient monuments are mysterious and not all mysterious monuments are ancient.

The Georgia Guidestones are decidedly *not* ancient—until 1980 there was nothing on top of that bare hill outside of Elberton, Georgia—yet there is much that is extremely mysterious about them.

Raymond Wiley and KT Prime do a first-class job in this little book of telling what is known about the stones, and what is not, revealing and exploring their mysteries one by one. They always keeps their feet on the ground and avoid extravagant or fanciful explanations when a simpler one will do. This only makes it all the more mysterious, after the ground has been so thoroughly raked over, that we still to this day do not know the true identity of the man calling himself R. C. Christian who commissioned and paid for the monument!

What is unmissable, is the strong whiff of seventeenth century Rosicrucianism running through the whole story; indeed the Guidestones bear many of the hallmarks of a "Rosicrucian stunt" in the classic mold designed to shake things up, challenge old and entrenched positions, get people thinking along new lines.

One night in 1623, for example, dramatic placards were positioned on the walls of many public buildings in Paris and distributed along all the main streets of the city. They contained pronouncements from the "deputies of the principal College of the Brothers of the Rose Cross who show and teach without books or marks how to speak all languages of the countries where we wish to be and to draw men from error and death." The placards also stated that the deputies were "making a visible and invisible stay in the city." In other words they would be seen only by those who they wished to see them, while to others they would be invisible.

The placards caused a "hurricane" of rumor about the mysterious Rose Cross fraternity and its eponymous founder Christian Rosenkreutz. Various Rosicrucian documents, espousing radical and far-reaching ideas, had already begun to circulate and hundreds more were to appear, going on to play a key role in the Enlightenment. Bizarrely, however, it was always also understood that Rosicrucianism—and certainly its core notion of a secret brotherhood of sages and savants waiting in the wings to take over the guidance of society—was something of a hoax and that the so-called Rosicrucian Manifestoes were allegorical in nature.

All this seems to me to fit perfectly with the strange story of the Guidestones, starting of course with the elusive funder "R. C. Christian" (i.e., Christian Rosenkreutz), who claims to represent a group of Americans who believe in God (like the original members of the Rosy Cross Brotherhood), who is visible to some in the Elberton community but not to others, and who creates a monument inscribed in multiple languages "to convey certain ideas across time [and to] hasten in small ways the dawning of an age of reason."

I suggest, however, that the ideas expressed in the stones' inscriptions, like the ideas in the original Rosicrucian Manifestoes, are there first and foremost to get people worked up emotionally and engaged intellectually with issues they might otherwise pass over. Thus, for example, the statement on the Guidestones that we should "Maintain Humanity Under 500,000,000" does not have to be in any way "true," or rooted in any great wisdom, or even something that "R. C. Christian" himself necessarily believed in, to fulfill the function of shaking up our thinking about global population and alerting us to the moral, ethical and other issues involved in enforced population control. Likewise the notion of a "world court" that appears on the Guidestones may be a piece of advocacy for such an institution, or it may again simply be intended to make us think.

To this extent the extreme reactions the monument has provoked, including the 2008 spray paint and polyepoxide attack, could be exactly what "R. C. Christian" and his shadowy group hoped for and intended when they conceived of and commissioned the Guidestones. To attack something in the realm of ideas one must first get to grips with it and try to understand it. As we do this, though it may be subtle at first, it can begin to shape and change us.

What better form of initiation is there than the one that leads us to initiate ourselves?

GRAHAM HANCOCK is the author of *Fingerprints of the Gods* and *Supernatural*, and co-author, with Robert Bauval, of *The Master Game*.

2. The Flagstone

CHAPTER 1:

THE GEORGIA GUIDESTONES

It was a slow day at the Elberton Granite Finishing Company. In the sleepy, North Georgia town of Elberton, most days were slow, even in the region's busiest industry, but this day was especially slow. It was a Friday afternoon in June of 1979. No one seems to know which Friday it was anymore, but it was definitely slow—Joe H. Fendley Sr., the president of EGFC, would remember that much at least because, apart from the secretary, he was the only one in the office.

The man who walked in was, according to Fendley, "neatly dressed" and "middle-aged."[1] He introduced himself with what would later be revealed as a pseudonym, and he told the businessman that he needed to commission a granite monument. Thinking that this man, like many others before him, was looking to buy a simple tombstone, Fendley courteously informed the gentleman that his company did not fill orders for private citizens, but only dealt in bulk with other corporate entities.

But for reasons unstated, "Robert Christian" had decided to do his business with EGFC, and he would not be turned away so easily. He told Fendley that what he was interested in creating was no mere memorial, but a "monument to the conservation of mankind,"[2] and he outlined the details of what he had envisioned.

What the enigmatic man proposed was truly massive. He wanted to create a structure that would require the quarrying of several enormous pieces of granite. He wanted it to be erected in such a mathematically precise way that they would require both engineers and astronomers to ensure it was done properly. Nothing of this magnitude had ever been attempted in Elbert County, and Elbert County prided itself on its vast experience with granite. The project Christian proposed was going to cost an extraordinary amount of money.

When Fendley heard these specifications, his interest piqued somewhat, but he was now uncertain as to whether or not the stranger was actually serious in his request. He quoted a very high price to Christian, and stressed that even that was just an estimate, as "no monument of this size had ever been quarried in Elberton."[3] To Fendley's great surprise, this did not seem to deter the mysterious man. Christian merely asked him for a reference to a local bank, and once he had it, left as quickly as he had come.

Not long thereafter, at the nearby Granite City Bank, bank president Wyatt C. Martin also received a most unusual visit. The same strange man walked into Martin's office and introduced himself as "Robert C. Christian," but again he admitted that this was not his real name. He explained to the bank manager that he was looking to commission a granite monument of considerable size. He repeated the details of the project to Martin.

In an interview with Randall Sullivan of *Wired* magazine in 2009, Martin confessed to being amazed by the stranger's request, and by the stranger himself. He tried to dissuade Christian from his intended project, echoing Fendley's concern that nothing so large had been produced in Elberton before, but again the well-dressed man was resolute. Christian indicated that he would return to see Martin the following week and "went off to charter a plane and spend the weekend scouting locations from the air."[4]

As promised, but nevertheless against expectation, R. C. Christian walked back into Martin's office that next Monday. The bank president, who had discussed the bizarre occurrence with Joe Fendley over the weekend and dismissed it as a hoax from a fellow Shriner, told Christian straight off that if they were really going to proceed, then he would need to know the man's identity. He had to have some assurance that the monument would be paid for. Christian seemed to understand this, and he agreed to reveal himself, but only under two conditions: Martin had to sign a non-disclosure agreement vowing never to reveal his name or information, and he had to promise to destroy all of the information pertaining to the project after its completion. The bank president agreed to the terms, and Wyatt C. Martin became the first and, so far, the only person to know the true identity of the mysterious Robert Christian.

After his second meeting with Wyatt Martin, Christian reentered Joe Fendley's office and delivered to him both a wooden scale-model of the landmark he was commissioning and a detailed set of building instructions. The very next Friday Martin telephoned Fendley to let him know that a

$10,000 deposit had been wired through, and Fendley began his work in earnest.

It was an enormous undertaking. Each of the four main stones that were cut from Joe Fendley's Pyramid Quarry was roughly twenty-eight tons in weight, and R. C. Christian had specified that the granite used had to be unblemished, which further complicated matters. It took the crew of quarrymen several weeks to remove each single stone from the earth. After their removal, the slabs of granite had to be cleaned and sized, and the more than 4,000 letters and characters of the Guidestones' message needed to be etched into their faces. The C. S. Peck Company developed an entirely new device to aid in the cleaning and sizing of these over-large stones. Project superintendant Joe B. Davis and his team spent nearly nine months at the previously abandoned Oglesby Granite shed preparing the pieces of the landmark that would make their town famous.

While the granite was being prepared, Wyatt Martin had to locate an appropriate site for the burgeoning monument. Christian had indicated that he wanted the stones placed in a "remote, wilderness area away from the main tourist centers."[5] This was not terribly difficult to accommodate. Elberton is a sleepy town in a quiet part of North Georgia and, until the Georgia Guidestones, did not have much in the way of a tourist center. While Christian had initially selected a site near Augusta, Martin persuaded him that a location closer to Elberton would be better, both because transporting the stones would be simpler, and because old Cherokee legends held that Elbert County was the center of the world.

So Martin scouted out three different potential sites in Elbert County for Mr. Christian to consider. The last site that he showed the mystery man was his own favorite on the list, and, as it turned out, also the one that most pleased the benefactor.

Seven miles north of Elberton, Wayne and Mildred Mullenix owned a five-acre plot of land adjacent to their family farm. One of the highest points in Elbert County, the plot sat atop a large hill and provided an open view of the surrounding farmlands, and the horizon, in all directions. The Mullenix family had been using the space as grazing land for their cattle, and in the purchase agreement worked out between the two parties, R. C. Christian agreed to allow them two generations of grazing rights. The deal was signed, and the future home of the Georgia Guidestones was chosen.

The specifications laid out by the monument's strange benefactor required that the stones' orientation with respect to the sun, the moon, and the stars be exact enough that the monument could be used both as a calendar and as a time-keeping device. Davis, who had come out of retirement to oversee this project, contracted engineers and even an astronomer from the University of Georgia[6] in order to ensure the precise placement of the foundations for the stones.

In all, the planning and construction of Elberton's most famous monument took almost a full year, but on March 22, 1980, on the vernal equinox, the Georgia Guidestones were finally revealed to the public for the first time.

When the long sheets of covering black plastic were

pulled away, the visitors were treated to quite a sight. Weighing a grand total of 237,746 pounds and composed of 951 cubic feet of granite, the Guidestones stand an impressive nineteen feet, three inches high overall. The central, "Gnomon" stone is roughly sixteen feet tall, three feet wide, and seven inches thick. It contains a hole at eye-level, drilled from the south to the north side in such a way as to allow the North Star to always be visible through it. Also cut into the Gnomon stone is a slot running from the west side to the east, through which a visitor during the summer or winter solstice could watch the sun rise.

Fanned out in an "X" about the Gnomon stone are four enormous upright slabs of granite that bear the message of R. C. Christian, the ten precepts, in eight different languages. Translators were employed from around the country, even from the United Nations,[7] in order to correctly display the ten tenets in Spanish, Swahili, Hindi, Hebrew, Arabic, Mandarin Chinese, and Russian in addition to English. These languages were selected, according to R. C. Christian, "for their historical significance and for their impact on people now living."[8] Each word in every language was carefully engraved into the granite by Charlie Clamp, a local sandblaster. Clamp would later report that during his work he heard "strange music and disjointed voices"[9] as he carved.

On the stone that points to the north, in English, the text of the Guidestones is as follows:

MAINTAIN HUMANITY UNDER 500,000,000
IN PERPETUAL BALANCE WITH NATURE

GUIDE REPRODUCTION WISELY –
IMPROVING FITNESS AND DIVERSITY

UNITE HUMANITY WITH A LIVING
NEW LANGUAGE

RULE PASSION – FAITH – TRADITION –
AND ALL THINGS
WITH TEMPERED REASON

PROTECT PEOPLE AND NATIONS
WITH FAIR LAWS AND JUST COURTS

LET ALL NATIONS RULE INTERNALLY
RESOLVING EXTERNAL DISPUTES
IN A WORLD COURT

AVOID PETTY LAWS AND USELESS
OFFICIALS

BALANCE PERSONAL RIGHTS WITH
SOCIAL DUTIES

PRIZE TRUTH – BEAUTY – LOVE –
SEEKING HARMONY WITH THE
INFINITE

BE NOT A CANCER ON THE EARTH –
LEAVE ROOM FOR NATURE –
LEAVE ROOM FOR NATURE

Sitting astride the other stones is the capstone. It is six and a half feet wide, nearly ten feet long and seven inches thick. A hole was drilled through the top of this stone in such a way as to allow the sun to shine through it and onto the southern face of the Gnomon stone. It was intended that the central stone would have markings on it that would allow one to determine the day of the year by observing exactly where the sunlight from this shaft hit the stone, but this feature has never been completed. Along the four outer faces of the capstone a message reads, "Let these be guidestones to an Age of Reason," in Classical Greek, Sanskrit, Egyptian hieroglyphics, and Babylonian cuneiform.

It is an impressive structure, taller than the average height of the megaliths at Stonehenge, and it was hoped that it would one day be more impressive still. R. C. Christian indicated that other stones could be "erected in the outer circles to mark the migrations of the moon and possibly other celestial events."[10] He left one-hundred leather-bound, signed copies of his book, *Common Sense Renewed*, in trust to the Georgia Guidestones Foundation with the understanding that they would be given to individuals who made contributions allowing those stones to be built. As yet, however, there have been no donations in amounts substantial enough to continue construction.

A few feet west of the monument, another granite slab lies set into the ground. This explanatory tablet provides information for visitors to the site about the dimensions and purpose of the extraordinary landmark. The heights and weights of all of the stones are indicated here, as well as the astronomical features built into the structure. Mention is made of a time capsule, which the Elberton Historical Society had originally intended to bury under the tablet, but the capsule was never placed, and so the information is enigmatically incomplete. The "author" of the monument is listed as, "R. C. Christian (a pseudonyn)" [*sic*]. The "sponsors" of the monument are listed as, "A small group of Americans who seek the Age of Reason."

When Christian presented himself to both Wyatt Martin and Joe Fendley, he indicated that he was not one man acting alone, but was a member of a "small group of loyal Americans who believe in God," who had been planning this for twenty years in order to "leave a message for future generations."[11] Ever since the erection of the monument, many individuals studying the Guidestones mystery have come up with a variety of theories as to the identities of both Christian himself and the group that he claimed to represent. But the only man who may have those answers with certainty is Wyatt Martin, and in the more than thirty years that have elapsed he has not chosen to reveal his secret. "I never did tell," Martin says, "and I never will. When I'm dead and gone, they'll never know."[12]

A crowd of more than four hundred people, many of them stonemasons and contractors instrumental in the building process, gathered on the treeless hill near the Mullenix farm to witness the unveiling ceremony. But if Robert Christian was among them, he did not make himself known. He did however, send a statement to be read during the ceremony, the contents of which he would later incorporate into the book that he would write and publish under the same pseudonym.

In both the book and the statement, Christian expressed great apprehension about the state of world affairs at that time. Facing the stark reality of the Cold War and the nuclear arms race between the United States and Russia, Christian and his group feared the worst. They, like many of their contemporaries, saw nuclear holocaust as the nearly inevitable result of the escalating hostilities. In response to this dark vision, they resolved to leave something behind for future generations to see after the radioactive dust cleared. They wanted to pass along a set of guidelines that they felt would prevent society from coming back to such a bleak point if they were followed.

In *Common Sense Renewed*, Christian more specifically lays out his ideas for a reformed society. He proposes solutions to problems like over-population, homelessness, foreign aggression, resource depletion, environmental deterioration and lack of education. Many of these problems, he postulated, could be readily solved, and perhaps the apocalypse could be staved off.

To ensure that his message was heard, Christian had copies of the first two editions of his book distributed in 1986 to "several thousand political officials and shapers of public opinion throughout the world. All members of the United States Congress received copies."[13] The third edition of the book, printed in 1990, after the fall of the Berlin Wall, makes brief mention in the foreword of the fact that many of Christian's hopes seem to have been actualized by world leaders. Whether or not they were influenced by *Common Sense Renewed*, however, remains unknown.

The excerpt that was read at the Guidestones unveiling ceremony did not go into nearly so much detail as did the 128-page tome. But it did convey to the assembled crowd that the stated purpose of the newly erected structure was to "outline in general terms certain basic steps which must be taken to establish for humanity a benevolent and enduring equilibrium with the universe."[14]

The statement was intended, no doubt, to clarify to the inhabitants of Elbert County, and to the public at large, the meaning of the monument's tenets and the intentions of its sponsors. But it did nothing to quell the storm that was to come, and it did nothing to dispel the fear and anxiety that many developed as a result of the sponsors' decision to leave their identities mysteriously unknown.

"Our message is in some areas controversial," the statement read. "We have chosen to remain anonymous in order to avoid debate and contention which might confuse our meaning and which might delay a considered review of our thoughts."

Without knowing the identities of the group members, it is impossible to say for certain whether that knowledge would have caused greater controversy than the mystery has. What is certain is that if the founders wished to avoid negative reactions and controversy in their entirety by preserving their anonymity, then in that respect they failed.

But the people of Elberton are still proud of their town's accomplishment. An exhibit on the Georgia Guidestones figures prominently at the front of the city's charming museum of granite, and in 1984, a one-third scale model of the stones was sent to Elberton's then sister-city, Mure, Japan. And the people involved in the project's creation seem to look upon it with a certain satisfaction.

A few months after the unveiling ceremony, Joe Fendley, now deceased, summarized his attitude toward the monument, remarking, "I think this is a unique thing for Elberton and the whole state. It is something we can all be proud of, and people will marvel at it centuries from now."[15]

Perhaps they will indeed last for centuries. The Guidestones still stand today, but they are marred. The graffiti has been scrubbed off, the signs have been removed, but the epoxy stains remain. And rumors continue to circulate and gather momentum on Internet message boards and in homes across the country. Strangely, as the years pass, the controversy surrounding the monument seems to grow only more vehement as the mystery endures.

3. Joe Fendley (left) and Wyatt Martin (right) with
R. C. Christian's wooden model of the Guidestones

4. Joe Fendley at the "Double 7" Ranch,
future site of the Guidestones

CHAPTER 2:

THE GRANITE CAPITAL OF THE WORLD

Northeast of Atlanta, a little over thirty miles beyond the university town of Athens, lies the tiny city of Elberton, Georgia. Founded in 1803, the town was originally named "Elbertville" after General Samuel Elbert, who fought in the American Revolutionary War. Today it is the county seat of Elbert County and the self-proclaimed "Granite Capital of the World," producing more granite monuments than any other city worldwide. But despite that distinction, it is a relatively quiet little town, hosting a population of only 4,546[16] within the four square miles of the city proper. It is not the kind of place that one would expect to be at the heart of a controversial mystery, but since the Georgia Guidestones were built in 1979, that is exactly what it has been.

The array of granite stones standing just off U.S. Highway 77 has drawn both criticism and acclaim from tourists who have come to visit it. Throughout the world, those who are aware of the monument have voiced opinions about it that cover a broad spectrum. Some have openly called for the "satanic" monument's destruction, while others believe that it should be protected as a beacon of peace. This extreme diversity of perspective also exists among the residents of Elbert County, Georgia, a microcosm of the wide world that surrounds it.

THE UNVEILING

The debate began almost immediately.

On March 22, 1980, Mayor Jack Wheeler and Rep. Doug Barnard, Jr. (D-GA) stood on a windy hill in northeast Georgia and cut a rope. Its binding gone, an enormous sheet of black plastic fell to the ground and revealed the new landmark it had been covering. Six slabs of solid granite, engraved with writings in twelve languages, towered above the gathered crowd. No one cheered.

The mayor and the congressman each spoke a piece about the monument. A passage from a letter written by the mysterious founder, R. C. Christian, was read to the crowd. Then William G. Hutton, who was at that time the president of the Monument Builders of North America, stepped forward to say a few words.

> The Guidestones are what may be one of the few lasting mementos of a civilization that some thousands of years hence may not exist. It would be very interesting to hear the remarks if some future resident of that far-off time, say in the year 3586, happens upon them and deciphers one or more of the stones and says something like, "I wonder what went wrong here?"[17]

The crowd shifted uncomfortably as he spoke. Though they had all read in the local paper that the purported purpose of the monument was to act as a beacon to survivors of a possible global catastrophe, not all of them believed this to be true. The sponsor's anonymity and the strange words etched into the stones had given rise to fear and suspicion in many hearts. There were rumors that the Guidestones had a more sinister meaning.

After the ceremony, the visitors had a chance to examine the new local attraction more closely. They milled about the site, sampling the refreshments provided and talking to the local reporters who had attended to cover the event. One man in particular drew a small crowd around him as he discussed his opinions with a writer from *Brown's Guide to Georgia*.

"Some of my congregation feel the same way I do," said the Reverend James Traffensted of the Elberton Church of God. "We don't think Mr. Christian is a Christian."[18] A few murmurs and nods from the people around him confirmed that this worry was shared.

> Look what it says about the unity of the world, especially with the world court. That's where the Antichrist will unite the governments of the world under *his* power, the power of the devil ... They seem so innocent in outward appearance, but the scripture teaches that there will be seducing spirits and doctrines of devils in the last days, according to Paul ... I think they will find this monument is for sun worshipers, for cult worship and devil worship.[19]

Traffensted, like some of the other Christians in Elberton, was very concerned by aspects of the monument that he perceived as satanic. The presence of foreign languages on the stones, the frequent references to nature, and the landmark's strong resemblance to Stonehenge all combined to present an unsettling image in the minds of some of the townsfolk.

As he was the only man to know the real identity of the Guidestones' strange backer, R. C. Christian, banker Wyatt Martin was often approached by the concerned citizens of Elberton who felt the monument was an "evil thing,"[20] especially in the early years. He did his best to set their minds to ease, but it was no simple task. "In the Bible," he explains, "we find instances where children were actually burned or killed in dedication to strange gods. And they had the idea this was going to happen up there ... But it was never meant for that."[21]

Regardless of the intentions of the founder, however, local pagan groups have held rituals at the site—though there is no evidence that there has ever been anything so dramatic as a human sacrifice anywhere on the grounds. There were even some local occultists present for the dedication ceremony. Self-described "psychic," Nonnie Wright Bakelder attended the unveiling specifically because she felt that there was something inherently magical about the site, but she did not see that as a bad thing. The land that the Georgia Guidestones stands upon, she claimed, has a "very high form of energy, a special energy—some would call it a vortex or a power spot."[22] According to Bakelder, this energy theoretically could be harnessed by a magician or witch and channeled into a ritual.

But, at least according to the official story, R. C. Christian did not select the location for the monument by himself.

Wyatt Martin claims that he himself sought out and found three potentially suitable properties and presented them to the mystery man as options. Of the three alternatives, Mr. Christian decided upon the pasture of Wayne Mullenix's Double Seven Ranch, but Martin insists that "any connection between the site chosen and occult indications is purely coincidental."[23]

But it was not the apparently "energetic" location that raised eyebrows with the locals. It was the actual guides on the Guidestones and even its overall design that caused alarm in some circles. An associate of Reverend Traffensted, the Reverend Cecil McQuaig claimed not long after the dedication that the monument was "beyond any doubt the work of a group dedicated to the ancient cult of the Egyptians, who used this type of structure for sun-worship."[24] The astronomical features of the stones, while reportedly designed to aid the survivors of a future cataclysm, are, for many Elberton Christians, too reminiscent of the structures built by early pagans. Equally troubling to McQuaig is the monument's overall resemblance to Stonehenge, as this suggests to him that it was designed for "occult worship of the Old Religion."[25]

As the stones themselves refrain from making any religious statements, either pagan or otherwise, those who visit the Guidestones are left to speculate as to whether or not R. C. Christian would be pleased by the pagan rites that have taken place around his creation. For his part, Wyatt Martin continues to believe that the man he met did not have witchcraft in mind when he made his plans. "I know Mr. Christian to be an honorable man who holds a responsible position in his community, and [is] respected by those who know him."[26]

A HOAX IN GRANITE

While some in the community have continued to insist that there is more to the story of R. C. Christian than is officially told, others suspect that the entire account is fictional. The story is admittedly an odd one—after all, it is not every day that a mysterious stranger walks into a small town and commissions a monument to "Reason." A few Elbertonians believe that it is extraordinary enough to be suspicious, and since before the first stone was quarried, rumors have circulated that the entire venture was merely a "promotional stunt"[27] and that "the Guidestones were created by a cabal of local merchants and the granite producers to boost tourism and to erect a self-serving monument to the quarryman's craft."[28]

If it all truly was a hoax, though, it was certainly an elaborate and expensive one. Dozens of quarrymen and granite workers labored for months to produce the stones, and the services of United Nations translators, astronomers, and mathematicians had to be contracted in order to ensure the accuracy of the design details. And while the exact cost of the production of the Guidestones has never been disclosed, it was certainly more expensive than the average small business' advertising campaign. Joe Fendley dismissed the theory with a laugh. "I'd think of a lot better ways to spend my money than this if I wanted to promote something."[29] Former member of the Elberton Granite Association, Hudson Cone, believes the same today. "They could've got a lot more bang for their buck using other more conventional marketing means," he says.

And if the R. C. Christian story was really a myth, then it would have to be Fendley and Martin who concocted it. They were the two men who reportedly had contact with the mysterious benefactor, and they had the deepest involvement with the creation of the monument. But those who actually knew them did not find it likely that they would fabricate such a story.

"I know him well enough," Wayne Mullenix said of Fendley, "so I don't think that this is any real gimmick or hoax or that Joe's behind it."[30] Even the granite man's employees did not find the idea terribly plausible. "Big Joe's too stingy,"[31] one of the quarrymen at his Pyramid Quarry said, refuting the theory. And the popular sentiment about Martin was similarly inclined. His customers at the bank found him to be a dependable and honest man. "Wyatt is straight and plain business," said one of the merchants with whom Martin regularly dealt. "He's not your mystery monument type."[32]

Hoax or no, the Georgia Guidestones have certainly been a boon to the granite industry and the area. Today it remains "the number one tourist attraction in Elbert County," according to the current mayor of Elberton, Larry Guest. Indeed all who visit can see the fine craftsmanship of the many hands that worked the stone.

ELBERTON'S LEGACY

Wyatt Martin believes that the biggest reason that the townsfolk have been so reluctant to accept the Guidestones is that the man who commissioned them remained anonymous. "The fact that they didn't know who put it there—that was the thing that was always the burr under their saddle,"[33] he says with a chuckle. There is a generally held expectation, especially in a small town, that business transactions will be handled in a transparent and public fashion, with a handshake to seal the deal. But R. C. Christian never even spoke to most of the people who were involved in his project, and for some of the locals this seemed like suspect behavior.

The tract of land that the mysterious stranger purchased as a home for the Guidestones was a five-acre plot of the pasture of Wayne Mullenix's family farm. Mullenix was among those who were put off by all the secrecy. "Selling my land to someone I never met and never will makes me wonder what's going on,"[34] he said. Those misgivings have remained in the hearts of some of the residents of Elbert County, though the Guidestones have stood for quite some time now. Some of the local preachers still deliver sermons about the "evil" landmark, and it gets very few visits from those in the local community.

But when the stones were vandalized in 2007, the community reacted strongly. Gary Jones, the current publisher of *The Elberton Star*, recalls that there was a "general feeling of disgust" from the locals at the idea that someone would try to destroy this piece of their history. The Elberton Sheriff's Department even went so far as to install surveillance cameras at the site to deter any others who wish harm to the property. "Those stones have stood there for thirty years without disturbing anyone," Jones says. "They are a good thing for the community."

Because even though some people in town remain apprehensive about it, the monument does still have many supporters in Elberton. "The place has a personality all its own," says Carolyn Cann, former weekly editor of *The Elberton Star*. "People are drawn there for a reason."[35] Cann has followed the Guidestones mystery since its beginnings, as she was the "ace reporter" for the coverage of the stones when they were built, according to Jones. And she has always believed that the words on the stones have a positive meaning. The man who sandblasted them into the granite agrees with her. "The sayings are all right," says Charlie Clamp. "If mankind would go by the Guidestones, I think we'd have a better mankind."[36]

The current mayor of Elberton, Joe Fendley's successor, is less sure of what to make of the strange stones so near to his town. The messages engraved into the monument "seem a little strange," says Mayor Larry Guest. "There's some things on there most people wouldn't agree with." In truth, even those who do not subscribe to the conspiracy theories that speculate that the Guidestones portend that an evil global government is on the rise could find reasons to disagree with a few of the tenets. And in a politically conservative area like Elberton, Georgia, they could find more than just a few.

"I don't know what those things are, and I don't want to know." A waitress at a local barbeque restaurant told a reporter on the day of the dedication. "The Russian's on 'em so that when the Russians invade us they'll have something to read."[37] As the structure was built during the Cold War, the inclusion of Russian in the languages into which the guides were translated was rather controversial at the time. The tenets' call for peace and for the resolution of international disputes with diplomacy rather than warfare was also not well-received in some circles. But the Cold War was also a time when the threat of massive atomic destruction on a global scale loomed ominously every day.

"This is something that would survive in the event of a nuclear war,"[38] countered George Gaines of the Elberton Granite Association at the unveiling ceremony. And if the Guidestones really were intended to stand as an aid to the survivors of that war, it would make sense for the guidelines it posited for civilization to have a more peaceful bent than the standard rhetoric of the day. "I think it is very great," said Edgar Allen Davidson, a Jamaican quarryman who helped remove from the earth the chunks of granite that would become the Guidestones. "The monument will make a change in people's lives. As days go by, people can see what the past days was."[39]

These days though, with the Cold War over, thoughts of a potential nuclear Armageddon are generally far from the townsfolk's minds. But the strange collection of stones remains, and with it its political sentiments. Many of the local residents do not agree with those ideas, and even Wyatt Martin himself has confessed to being somewhat put-off by the environmentalist sympathies expressed in the final tenet, "Be not a cancer on the Earth—Leave room for nature—Leave room for nature."

The Mullenix family too has its doubts about the intentions of the creator of the monument, but they are still proud when they look out their windows in the morning and see it standing there. "I'm glad to see it for Elbert County," says Wayne Mullenix's wife, Mildred. She, like the rest of the world, does not know what the Guidestones really mean, but she knows that they have been good for the area.

It has been over thirty years now since that crowd of hundreds first gathered together in the Mullenix pasture to catch a glimpse of the mystery stones, and much of the local controversy has died down. "It's become just another granite attraction,"[40] says Tom Robinson, Joe Fendley's successor as president of the Elberton Granite Finishing Company. Many of the attendees at the dedication ceremony have passed on now, and most of the rest have gone on to discussing other matters. "Interest in the Guidestones has waned in Elberton," Hudson Cone admits. Events like the recent vandalism occasionally bring it back to the forefront of the townsfolk's minds, but it is largely the outsiders now who passionately debate the meaning of the monument.

To the town of Elberton it now mainly means a quaint curiosity, and a source of income through the tourism it brings. "It means economic development for us," says Mayor Guest, "more people in our hotels and restaurants."

And for as long as its origins remain shrouded in secrecy and the unknown, it will likely remain the biggest reason for out-of-towners to visit the tiny city. Perhaps, as Mr. Christian hoped, it will remain an enigma forever. But there is also the chance that someday, someone will discover the answers to the questions that have been speculated upon for so long. "It's a mystery, and I love a mystery," says Carolyn Cann. "But I believe that sooner or later, the whole truth will come out."[41]

5. The "mail slot" marks the sunrise line on the winter and summer solstice

6. This shaft marks the position of
Polaris throughout the year

7. A shaft cut through the capstone marks
noontime throughout the year.

CHAPTER 3:
ROSES, ROSES, ROSES

The mystery that surrounds the Guidestones, its meaning and origins has drawn a surprisingly large amount of interest from men and women beyond the borders of Elbert County as well. People from outside of Georgia, and even outside of the United States, have spoken and written about the landmark, giving voice to opinions both positive and negative. Even singer-songwriter Yoko Ono has given her thoughts on the matter, contributing a sound-collage called "Georgia Stone" to the 1993 John Cage tribute album, *A Chance Operation*. For a granite monument outside a small rural town, the response has been somewhat unprecedented.

Many of those who have visited, or even just learned about, the Guidestones have quickly developed a fondness for the site. It seems to resonate strongly with a wide variety of people, especially among those with a mystical bent.

THE OLD RELIGION

On March 22, 1980, the Georgia Guidestones were revealed for the first time to a crowd of onlookers. An unveiling ceremony was held in the morning, and several local political officials and businessmen spoke a few words to commemorate the event. But after the crowd had dispersed, a few individuals stayed behind. Among them were Jodi and John Minogue, two self-described "witches" from the Atlanta area. They lingered until the others had gone home, and then they performed a ceremony of their own at the monument.

Jodi changed into a long, purple robe and retrieved a sword and a vial of sandalwood oil from her car. She drew a circle around the perimeter of the new landmark, and then she and her husband John inscribed pentagrams on the faces of each of the stones with the oil. They chanted and walked about the stones two times, "once to banish negative forces, and again to invoke positive ones."[42] Believing the site to be a location of great power, Jodi stated that they performed the ritual because they wanted to cause the stones to "channel good and healing earth energy"[43] so that they would have a positive impact on the area and on the world. "I certainly see this as some sort of center for occult activity,"[44] she told reporters that day. But unlike many of the people today who share that opinion, Jodi did not consider that to be a bad thing.

Jodi and John belong to just one of the many pagan groups who have used the Guidestones as a site for their rituals in the time since their unveiling. The reasons that these groups believe the monument to be a sacred or magical site are manifold. The first and most obvious reason is that many groups practicing nature-based religions have felt a kinship between their own beliefs and the tenets written on the stones. Many Western neo-pagan traditions focus heavily on the need to revere and respect the earth, and the Guidestones—especially the final tenet's exhortation to "Leave room for nature"—seem to echo that sentiment.

The Minogues in particular have also discovered another feature of the monument that leads them to believe that it has magical significance. The physical location of the Guidestones seems to them to present a strangely large number of occurrences of the number seven. The landmark is located on U.S. Highway 77, which winds seven miles back to Elberton and is crossed by Georgia 17. The hill upon which the stones stand is roughly 750 miles above sea level. The parcel of land that R. C. Christian purchased to be the home of his strange project is the pasture of Wayne Mullenix's Double Seven Ranch. Even the dimensions of the major stones point to a seven: they are five meters tall and two meters wide, and when summed these numbers yield seven. The number seven, Mrs. Minogue asserts, is very magically important. It "stands for the mystic, the initiate. It is the number showing attainment of occult knowledge."[45] Other numbers containing seven are also meaningful, she continues; "seven-seven-seven is the representation for 'God Supreme,' and seventeen, the number of the highway connecting Elberton to the outside world, stands for guidance of a new era for mankind in the tarot."[46]

There are also other aspects of the location of the Guidestones that Jodi finds remarkable.

> The relation of the central stone to the sun and the moon show solar and lunar orientation, the male and female principles of the Old Re-

> ligion. It's also located on the cross-section of three energy points: there's a water line running north to south ... and there are underground lines of magnetic energy, and track-lines used by animals.[47]

The monument is also very near the spot that a southeastern Native American tribe, the Cherokee, called the center of the world. Just eight miles away, in what is now Hartwell, Georgia, a plaque on the side of the highway marks the place, "A-Yeh-Li-A-Lo-Hee" as the Cherokee themselves referred to it. It is uncertain now why exactly they felt that this particular place was so central, but the many old trails that radiate out from it provide a reasonable explanation. The proximity to this so-called *navel of the world*, coupled with the other evidence she sees, however, indicates to Jodi that the founder of the Guidestones had magical intentions in mind when he chose his location. "Mister Christian certainly seems to have known exactly what he was doing in laying out this monument,"[48] she asserts.

ARCHEOASTRONOMY

Randall Carlson, the owner of the website *Sacred Geometry International*, has also been interested in the Guidestones for many years because of the magical significance that he sees in the physical properties of the structure. A professional builder who has spent over forty years researching the mysteries that surround ancient ruins, Carlson developed a fascination with Elberton's mystery monument because it incorporates elements of what he calls "archeoastronomy"[49] into its design.

Carlson describes his primary interest, archeoastronomy, as archeological study that focuses on the theory that many of the ruins of ancient structures that have been uncovered in modern times were originally "built to reflect the Heavens." This seems to be a relatively simple and unthreatening idea, but Carlson contends that many other scholars are not comfortable with it. Modern historians are often inclined to portray ancient peoples as comparatively ignorant in the fields of mathematics and the sciences, he asserts, but the investigations of archeoastronomers seem to "suggest that people were much more sophisticated intellectually than the dogmatic models would acknowledge." In order to precisely "reflect star maps" with the architecture of a monument or set of monuments—such as Carlson suggests was done by the ancient Pueblo people in the tenth century at Chaco Canyon in northwestern New Mexico—the builders would have to know a great deal about astronomy and mathematics.

In the course of his work, Randall Carlson has studied a wide variety of medieval and ancient sites, but the Georgia Guidestones seem out of place in his research, as they were only built within the last century. What drew him to Elberton's mysterious stones was the fact that he perceived a great deal of similarities between the new monument and the older structures that he has been investigating for thirty years.

The cathedral in Chartres, France, for example, has an

interesting analogue to the calendrical system of the Guidestones that may indeed have been R. C. Christian's inspiration for adding such a feature to his monument. In the Cathedral of Our Lady of Chartres, there is a stained glass window that depicts the life of Saint Apollinaire within which there is a single clear pane of glass. Each year at high noon on the summer solstice, and at no other time, a ray of sunlight shines through this pane and falls directly on a nail that is set into an irregular rectangular flagstone on the floor. Carlson points out that this phenomenon is quite similar to the hole that is drilled into the capstone of the Guidestones monument which was intended to indicate the day of the year by directing a ray of light to the central column.

The Guidestones also have a connection to the summer solstice in the slot that pierces the central column. Through that slot, an onlooker can watch the sun rise on the summer solstice. Carlson has observed similar solsticial and equinocular alignments in "numerous" ancient structures that he has studied in the course of his research. And it was because of these features in the Guidestones, that he developed an interest in the monument.

Much like ancient ruins such as Stonehenge and the Chaco Canyon Complex, the Georgia Guidestones has the ability to act as both a solar and a lunar calendar by virtue of its very architecture. This physical connection between earthly bodies and heavenly ones seems to Carlson to speak of a "magical mindset"[50] on the part of the architects, in this case, R. C. Christian.

Both historically and in modern times, the phrase "as

above, so below" has been prevalent in occult and new age ideologies. At its roots a hermetic concept, the first occurrence of which is found in *The Emerald Tablet of Hermes*, a medieval alchemical text, where it appears as: "What is below is like that which is above; and what is above is like that which is below: to accomplish the miracle of the one thing."[51] This is meant as more than a general observation, however; it is also a kind of simplified definition of hermetic magic. It implies that things which are done on a symbolic, or small, scale have a proportional effect on a large, or global scale. And it is largely based upon this principle that many magical practitioners like the Minogues have speculated that for the anonymous Mr. Christian, the building of the Guidestones was, in and of itself, a magical act designed to bring about change on a global scale, purely by making a change on a small scale.

The particular change that the mysterious man wanted to elicit is debatable, but many have speculated that it was related to the tumultuous time-period during which the Guidestones were built, the Cold War. There were many fears at the time that the conflict between the United States and the Soviet Union would eventually erupt into a full-scale nuclear war that would lead to the end of civilization, and some believe that the Guidestones were built as insurance against that possibility. "The Guidestones," Jodi claims, "are to be a guide for humanity after the apocalypse."[52] She believes that R. C. Christian and the group he claimed to represent were looking after the best interests of humanity in the wake of potential catastrophe, and that they were doing so because they were Rosicrucians.

THE BROTHERHOOD OF R. C.

Between 1614 and 1615, two very strange anonymous manuscripts that would later become collectively known as the *Rosicrucian Manifestos* began to circulate around Germany. Their source was unknown, and their content claimed to announce the existence of a secret group of Christian magicians and mystics that had until that point never been made known to the public. Their circulation spread like wildfire, and soon the whole of Western Europe was abuzz with interest in these mysterious essays.

The first document was distributed under the title, *Fama Fraternitatis de R. C.*, which has been roughly translated to mean the "Discovery of the Brotherhood of R. C." Addressed to the "Learned in General and the Governors of Europe,"[53] the short pamphlet tells the story of a German referred to only as Brother C. R. C. In the tale, the man travels to the Middle East and learns quite a bit of information about science, mathematics, and magic that was at the time unknown in the West. He spends many years in these travels, and then he returns to Europe, hoping to share his new knowledge. But instead of being welcomed gratefully, he is scorned and reviled as foolish by the educated men of Europe, reportedly because they are unwilling to admit that there is so much that they did not know. Having failed to immediately reform the current course of science in the mainstream, he returns to Germany and gathers a small group of men—at first just three others, but later seven—together to found a society called the "Fraternity of the Rosie Cross."[54]

Together these men build themselves a temple, the

Sancti Spiritus, and develop a magical system of writing, in which they claim to have written many texts. The new brothers swear an oath to their order wherein they promise, among other things, to heal the sick free of any charge and to keep the fraternity secret for one hundred years. It is then revealed in the manuscript that the authors are the third generation of this fraternity, and that—the mandated one-hundred-year period of silence having ended—they are seeking to broaden their membership. Mysteriously, however, the manuscript provides no means for an interested party to contact this brotherhood.

The second pamphlet, which is mentioned by name in the first, is the *Confessio Fraternitatis R.C*, or the "Confession of the Brotherhood of R. C." Unlike the *Fama*, the *Confessio* is not a narrative tale of a legendary figure, but instead it merely expands upon the philosophy and workings of the group. Portions of this second document are structured apologetically, reasserting the claim made in the *Fama* that they are devout followers of Jesus Christ in the wake of public criticism of the first document. But other sections make bolder statements, decrying both the Roman Catholic Pope and Mahomet for their "blasphemies,"[55] and in the preface referring to the Pope as the "Antichrist."[56]

The *Confessio* also reiterates the desire of the brotherhood to recruit new members now that they feel the world has grown more progressive, but once again no clear means is presented to the reader who would seek application to the order. Instead, it is hinted that persons who are worthy to join the brotherhood will be found by the authors, and that all others will simply find nothing at all:

> A thousand times the unworthy may clamour, a thousand times may present themselves, yet God hath commanded our ears that they should hear none of them, and hath so compassed us about with His clouds that unto us, His servants, no violence can be done; wherefore now no longer are we beheld by human eyes, unless they have received strength borrowed from the eagle.[57]

Unsurprisingly these enigmatic manifestos caused quite a stir in Europe. According to historian Frances Yates, the "announcements aroused at the time a frenzied interest and many were the passionate efforts to reach the R. C. brothers by letters, printed appeals, and pamphlets. A river of printed works takes its rise from these manifestos, responding to their invitation to get into touch with the writers and co-operate with the work of the order."[58] Other writings, inspired by the pamphlets, began to crop up in cities around the continent, including one that claimed to be a third manifesto.

In 1616, a text entitled the *Chymical Wedding of Christian Rosenkreutz* appeared in Strasbourg. Divided into seven sections, the *Chymical Wedding* is a symbolic tale of Brother C. R. C.'s attendance at a wedding of a king and a queen. In the story, C. R. C. is referred to by the name Christian Rosenkreutz, a moniker that had not been applied to the legendary figure prior to this publication. The narrative is allegorical however, and actually seems to refer to an alchemical process whereby two disparate elements are joined rather than a true wedding between two people. This sort of structure was common among alchemical texts of the time period, and thus the text was readily believed to be genuine by the public.

However, several years later, a German theologian by the name of Johannes Valentinus Andreae published an autobiography in which he asserted that the document was a hoax. In his book, Andreae claimed authorship of the *Chymical Wedding* and stated that he had written it as "a *ludibrium*, or a fiction, or a jest, of little worth."[59] Since the publication of the original two manifestos, many had already speculated that perhaps the entire legend of the Brotherhood of the Rose Cross was merely a fabrication, and Andreae's allegation only added further fuel to that fire.

To this day it is still unclear whether or not the fraternity ever actually existed as such. Yates asserts that she has "found no evidence of a real secret society calling itself 'Rosicrucian', and really in existence as an organized group at the time the manifestos were published and during the time of the furore."[60] No actual persons were ever identified as certain members of the order, though many men attempted to contact and join the group. For historians it has become nearly impossible to even determine which, if any, of the hopefuls were actually earnest in their desires to become brothers, as so many of those who published open letters to the fraternity in the newspapers were "merely attracted by the exciting possibility of getting into touch with mysterious personages possessing superior knowledge or powers, or angered and alarmed by the imagined spread of dangerous magicians or agitators."[61]

But if the manifestos were not completely genuine in their presentation of their purpose, it is somewhat difficult to determine what purpose they could truly have served. Scholars have conjectured that they were perhaps intended allegorically, or that they were designed to illuminate the public as to the existence of similar hidden magical societies without specifically disclosing any details about them. It is also possible that the first two documents were, like the *Chymical Wedding* is now presumed to be, simply an elaborate joke.

The only thing that is known for certain is that the *Fama* and the *Confessio* continued to circulate throughout Europe for many years, and that their impact was far-reaching. In particular, the manifestos had an enormous effect on the development of other secret societies within Europe, most notably the Freemasons.

Though the Freemasons are a secret society and therefore not all the particulars of their history have become public knowledge, some of the details of their origin are a matter of record. One of the earliest people known to have been inducted into the Freemasonic order was a British antiquarian by the name of Elias Ashmole. Ashmole is notable in his early connection with the Freemasons largely because of his involvement with the Rosicrucian legend. He was one of the strongest initial supporters of the nebulous fraternity and he copied out in his own hand the *Rosicrucian Manifestos*, adding to them a formal letter admiring their aims and asking to be allowed to join."[62]

Other, more concrete factors seem to link the Freemasons to the Rosicrucian movement even more strongly. In early Masonic literature there are numerous references to the symbols utilized in the manifestos, some of which even mention the order by name. "For we be brethren of the Rosie *crosse*,"[63] proclaims an early Masonic poem, making it seem rather clear that even if they were not technically affiliated with the Brothers R. C., they were at least heavily inspired by them.

And in modern Scottish Rite Masonry, that influence remains in the symbolic language of the order. There is even a rank within the hierarchical structure of the order that conveys the title "Knight of the Rose Cross." Today there are a variety of magical societies, such as the Ancient Mystical Order Rosae Crucis (AMORC), that purport to be directly descended from the authors of those manifestos. For scholars and curiosity-seekers alike though, it is impossible to either confirm or deny such claims.

The Georgia Guidestones, however, would seem far removed from Renaissance legends. But there are those who make the claim that the Rosicrucians and the mysterious Elberton monument have more in common than at first it might appear.

For her part, Jodi Minogue says that she has "always ... speculated that 'R. C. Christian' stood for Rosicrucian."[64] She makes this connection because of a portion of the oath that the Brothers were mentioned to have taken in the *Fama Fraternitatis*, "that the word R. C. should be their seal, mark, and character."[65] And she is not alone in perceiving this correlation.

Randall Carlson also notes that "there seems to be Rosicrucian symbolism woven through the structure in various ways." He sees a possible correlation between the eight modern languages that are present on the Guidestones and the eight original Rosicrucian brothers. And to Carlson and many others who are familiar with the Rosicrucian legend, the pseudonym chosen by the Georgia Guidestones' mysterious creator presents "an immediate red flag."[66]

For though the body of Rosicrucian literature associates the group with a wide variety of symbols and signs, as Yates notes, "the emblem of the order is neither a double cross, a Fleece, or a Garter, but the words R. C."[67] This, coupled with the uncertainty surrounding the anonymous stranger's pseudonym, has led many to assume that the Guidestones' founder chose his name because he "was trying to align himself with the Rosicrucians."[68] For while Wyatt Martin reports that the stranger claimed to have chosen the last name "Christian" to highlight his own religious beliefs, he never made any comment as to why he chose the initials "R. C."

Many of those who subscribe to the theory that R. C. Christian was a member of a Rosicrucian order do not believe, however, that there is anything wrong with that. Quite to the contrary, among most pagans and occultists, the Rosicrucians have a very positive reputation. They are known for their belief in the importance of good works and charity, and the modern organizations profess to be dedicated largely to the idea of personal growth and improvement.

THE MASTER OF THE ROSE

In February of 1997, another mysterious stranger found his way to Elberton, Georgia on a mission. But this man did not go to the Elberton Granite Finishing Company, nor to the Granite City Bank, instead he went straight into the offices of Carolyn Cann. At that time, Cann was the weekly editor of the local newspaper, *The Elberton Star*, and had followed the events surrounding the Georgia Guidestones mystery very closely.

The man, who never revealed his identity, went to Cann to persuade her to become the caretaker of a trust that he wanted to set up to beautify the property that the Guidestones stood upon. The man insisted that the monument should present itself as more of a "Christian-oriented prayer site."[69] She consented, though she was confused as to why she had been singled out for this task, and the man donated a quantity of money sufficient to allow for the planting of rose bushes around the monument. He then submitted an article to her describing in detail his motivations for donating his money and promised to return soon to furnish the funds required to place benches at the site.

Cann never heard from him again, but a copy of the article that the mystery man wrote is still on file at the Elberton Public Library, and it provides further insight into his own theories as to the true meaning behind the Georgia Guidestones. Describing itself as "Article One of a Series," the text is titled "The Georgia Guidestones Guides the Stone," and it is here reproduced in its entirety:

What is the mystery? Does it point the way to a new age or to an old age returning? What is "THE COMING AGE OF REASON?" Why did the benefactor call himself R. C. Christian? Why was he anonymous? What did he know about what or WHO was to come? Why is the use of Granite Rock important? Is there a technical reason the Guidestones are constructed from granite? If so, what are the reasons? Why Blue Granite?

Why did Master Jesus say he would build his church "On The Solid Rock." Was it literal? Is that "solid rock" the solid granite of The Piedmont Region and the granite outcropping? Where is the center point of the outcropping and does it extend outward like a pebble in a pond or like radio waves?

We are told that "in the beginning was the word." Could it be that at the turn of the century is a new beginning and that the Georgia Guidestones are like a great key that turns the wheels of a clock to reset time. Could it be that there are clues in the word to point or guide the way to a new understanding that is contained within the word?

Words and sound go together like guidestones and guides the tone.

Words and sound go together like stone mountain and tone mountains.

Was it not sound that brought the wall of Jericho down?

Will not sound and frequency shatter a kidney stone and heal disease?

Cannot a beautiful soprano voice shatter glass with the purity of her tone or tender the woundings [*sic*] of a suffering soul with the same tone?

What is the relationship between the Georgia Guidestones, Stone Mountain, and the Piedmont Granite Shelf? Does it truly Guide the Tone, and Tone the Mountain? Are they not all "The Solid Rock." Is solid granite rock not also crystalline formation? Is not crystalline formation required in the transmission of sound waves and tone in the transmission of frequency and radio waves?

Is it coincidence that the Georgia Guidestones can be accessed by travelling through Hart

(Heart) County? Did not Master Jesus give his Heart to the Earth? And is not Heart and Earth the same word when the first (H) becomes the last Heart/earth?

WHAT DOES IT ALL MEAN! COULD IT BE THAT THE MYSTERY OF THE GEORGIA GUIDESTONES POINTS TO THE GREATEST MYSTERY OF ALL!

The Georgia Guidestones must become a sacred place. It is placed there for a very specific technical, religious, and geometric and astronomical reason. A great garden of life life life, life more abundant, life must be planted there with evergreens and roses roses roses, roses red, roses white for the blue rose to come.

"IF YOU BUILD IT! HE WILL COME!" A beautification and care fund has been set up by an anonymous benefactor into which all Christians are invited to contribute in the name of Jesus The Christ, The Savior of Mankind, The Greatest Master of Time itself. The endowment fund will be solely dedicated to the care of the garden that is to be built for the Great Master.

Many will begin to meet the Miraculous at

> the Stones That Guide and Miracles will meet those who come to the Garden To Pray for Guidance like the Great Master once prayed at Gethsemane before the Great Resurrection and Ascension. Miracles will come upon the wind. Miracles will come upon Sun that Rises. Miracles will come in the song of the bird. Great healings will begin to occur there.
>
> REMEMBER! "THE SOLID ROCK!"
>
> I will continue to unfold the mystery in articles presented to and through The Elberton Star. It is the Star in the East and I am simply a friend of THE MASTER OF THE ROSE.
>
> You may send your non profit donations or endowments to Carolyn Cann at the Elberton Star who has been asked to manage the beautification project to bring the Garden into Being and make the Stones that Guide a Sacred and far less mysterious place.

To date, no other donors, Christian or otherwise, have come forward to add to the beautification fund, and a single, bedraggled rose vine is all that remains of the roses that were planted "for the blue rose to come." But that rose and the mimeographed copy of the anonymous man's article remain as reminders of the clearly profound effect that Elberton's most mysterious monument had on at least one man.

THE SOCIETY OF THE THIRD MILLENNIUM

Over the years since their installation, the Georgia Guidestones have inspired a wide variety of people to take action. Some have felt compelled to perform ceremonies to honor the stones or to "channel" whatever power they believe them to possess, while others have sought to beautify the land on which the monument stands. And on one particular occasion, a group of individuals who perceived the message of the Guidestones to be in line with their own ideologies were moved to use the site as a platform on which to make a political statement.

On the morning of May 8, 2011, visitors to the Georgia Guidestones were shown a monument that was startlingly different from the one that had stood at the site since 1980. Each of the stones was draped with a black drop cloth that had been cut to its measure and inscribed on all sides with text in white paint. Atop the capstone, five small satellite dishes were affixed, each bearing a different phrase. The words written on the display were strange and confusing to the people of Elbert County, and no one seemed entirely certain what the demonstration meant. But a few days later, *The Elberton Star* received a letter from an organization calling itself "The Neo-Transcendentalists for the Society of the Third Millennium," who claimed credit for the installation.

In the letter, the Society of the Third Millennium, or S3K, referred to the new face they had given the Guidestones as "an outdoor, site-specific, guerilla art project called 'THE MONOLITHIC MILESTONES PROJECT, 2010–2011, A Declaration For Interdependence Through The Integral Vision, Strategy & Philosophical Pillars Of Neo-Transcendentalism At The Georgia Guidestones.'" The purpose of the project, they indicated, was to raise public awareness of their group and others like it that were attempting to foment sweeping social, cultural, and political change in order to achieve a state that they perceived would be better for mankind.

The Society of the Third Millennium is an anonymous organization. In their dealings with the public, its members each take on pseudonyms with the initials "ZXC," after the style of their leader, Zoren X. Cross. Though they more frequently describe themselves as "Neo-Transcendentalists," S3K also self-identifies as an organization composed of people who fit into the segment of the population known as "cultural creatives." Coined by psychologist, Sherry Ruth Anderson, and sociologist, Paul H. Ray, the term "cultural creative" describes a member of a movement first identified in the late 1990s. They are dissatisfied with the current state of geopolitics and active in trying to change them. Members of this group are generally highly concerned with environmental and social issues, and they believe that the current political systems are unable to adequately address those issues.

On their installation at the Georgia Guidestones, the Society of the Third Millennium explained at length their particular motivations, ideals, and goals. Four of the satellite dishes atop the capstone each bore the names of a group of people to whom they were directing their message—"New Progressives," "Green Conservatives," "The Millennials," and "Cultural Creatives"—while the final one indicated what they wanted to bring about: "The Grand Synthesis." Each face of the four main stones—which, uncovered, display R. C. Christian's ten tenets in different languages— showcased a different "pillar" of Neo-Transcendentalism. But the side that they marked as the "Philosophical Pillar" of "Foundational Principles" was perhaps the most informative in explaining the ideals of the group:

THE TEN TENETS FOR TRANSFORMATION

1. Perceptions no longer corresponds [*sic*] to reality so it becomes moral responsibility [*sic*] of the mentally liberated to help others break out of Matrix of False Consciousness [*sic*].

2. There is an absence of new modes of thinking that is Required to provide alternatives to the status quo. Only Cohesive Vision & Coherent Strategy Will Create & Capitalize Critical Mass For Transformative Change.

3. We Need To Envision Real Utopias & Develop A Common Code of Ethical Conduct Consis-

tent w/ the Various Basic Needs & Human Nature Tendencies.

4. Human Nature Is Not Greedy, Selfish, Aggressive & Individualistic, Instead The Tendency Is To Fit Into A Social Whole. Our Prehuman Ancestors Were Strongly Bonded, Sharing & Communal: the Building Blocks of "EARTH COMMUNITY." Thus "Nuturant [*sic*] Parent" Worldview coincides most with Human Nature.

5. In contrast, "Strict Father Figure" worldview perceives World [*sic*] As Evil & In Need To Be Protected From [*sic*] At All Cost & By whatever Violent, Dominating & Destructive Means available, like Torture, Oppression & War. This Has Led To Possessive Individualism, Extreme Competition, Excessive Materialism & the Ascendency of private property, Capital & Interest, Efficiency of Production Imperialism. The Corrupt Cornerstones of "EMPIRE."

6. While The Past cannot Be Undone, There Is No Moral Justification for ongoing exploitation into the future. It can Be halted only by understanding its past & present realities.

7. To bring about a more just world, major po-

litical changes Will be necessary. Politics is either the means for enforcing Those beliefs & assumptions, or the means for changing Them. Gov't, therefore, should not be perceived as "A Necessary Evil." But [*sic*] As The Physical Manifestation Of Our Highest Ideals.

8. However, Our Current Political System Is Broken. We Are Governed By A Plutocracy—Rule By The Elite Few.

9. Violence Must Be Avoided At All Costs, For The Ends Do not justify the means because the Means are the Ends In The Making. Ethics Is Not Doing What Is Best For the Most, But Instead Doing What Is Best For The Long Run.

10. Ultimately Our Power Lies Not With Working Within The System but By Unplugging The System Itself Through A Nationwide, General Strike That Will Require Courage, Sacrifice & Perseverance.

[*Original capitalization preserved.*]

When asked to comment as to why the group chose the Georgia Guidestones for their art installation, S3K member Zevin X. Cruz said that the notoriety of the stones was undeniably a factor, in that it was likely to generate more press for the organization. But he also said that what they perceived as the "secular humanist philosophy" of the Guidestones was seen by many in the organization as directly in line with the beliefs and motivations of their own group. Because of this, they took pains to ensure that the monument was not in any way damaged or permanently altered by their display. They drew inspiration from the stones as a "terrific work of art," and could think of no more fitting site to house their message.

The effect the Georgia Guidestones have had on others throughout the world has at times, however, produced a far less favorable impression. There are those who believe that the monument is not a symbol of the power and benevolence of "Master Jesus" or of grand social change, but of the tyrannical plans of a sinister and secretive group. And while these men and women were also moved to make alterations to the land that the Guidestones stand upon, it was not "beautification" or temporary change in the name of activism that they had in mind, but vandalism.

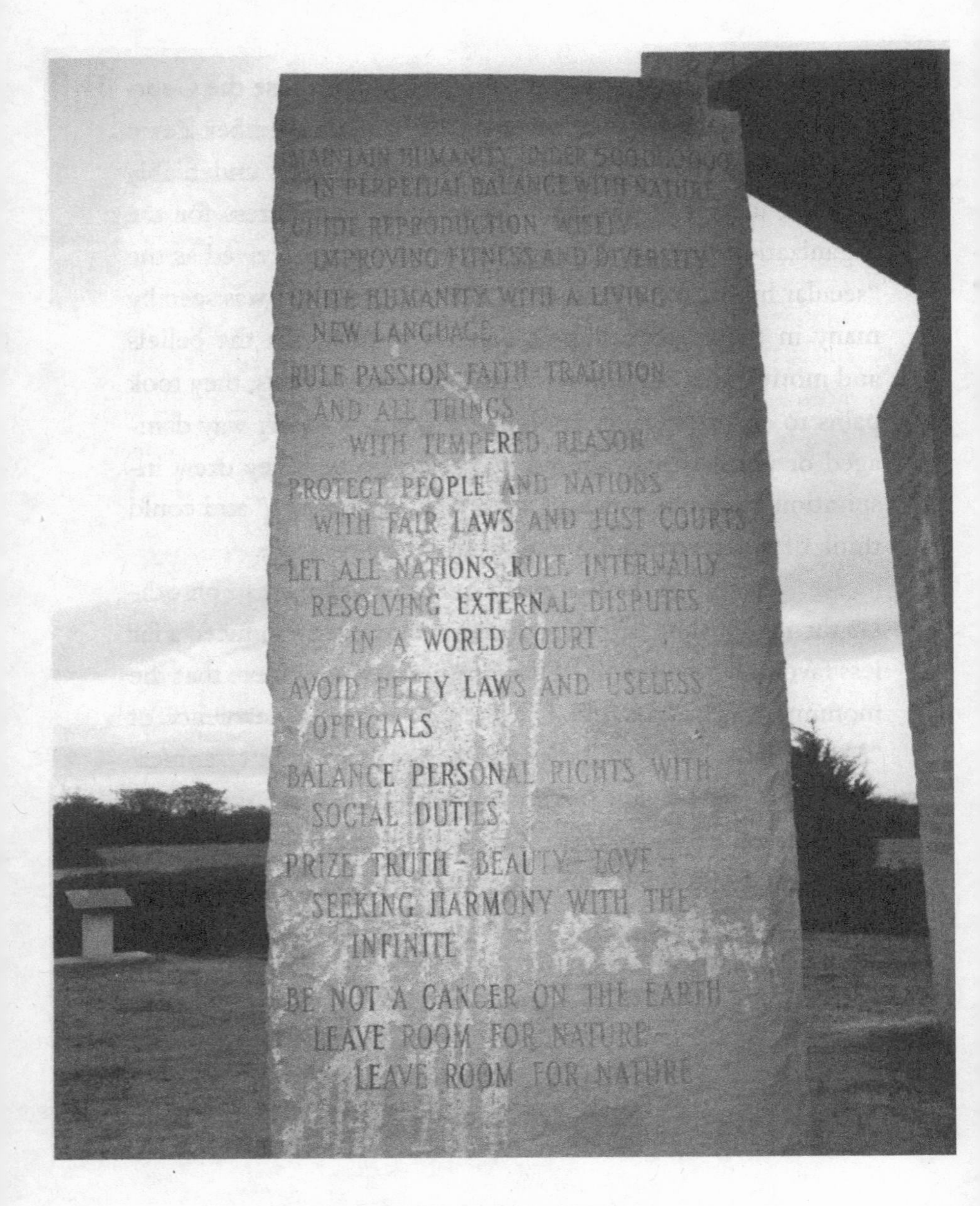

8. Epoxy damage to the English face

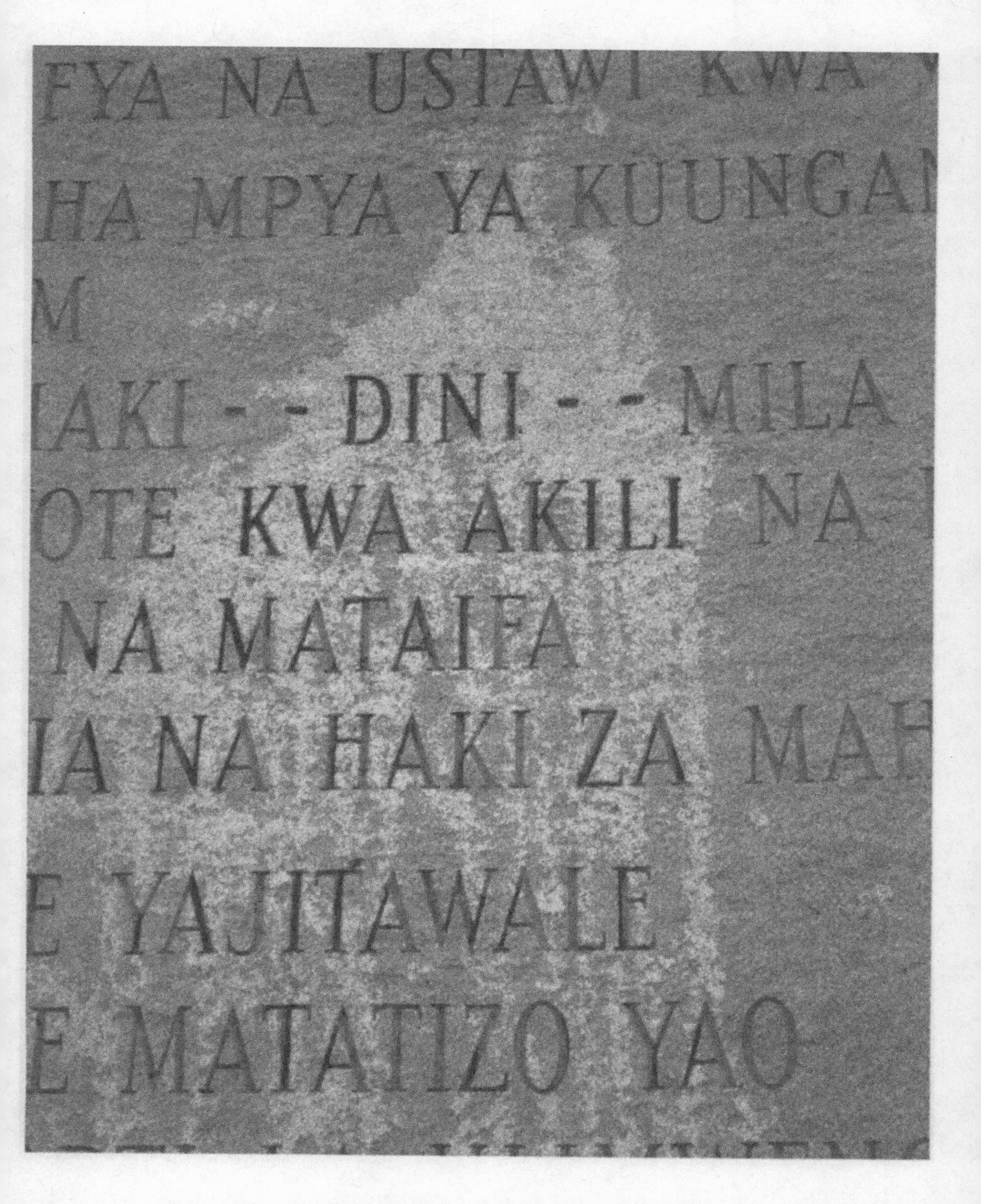

9. Epoxy damage to the Swahili face

10. Damage to flagstone, caused by treasure hunters digging for the time capsule

CHAPTER 4:
THE NEW WORLD ORDER

Not all of the speculation about the meaning and origins of the Georgia Guidestones has been favorable. To many people, the vague wording of the monument's text seems ominous, and the anonymity of its creator suspect. Far from considering the landmark to be a positive icon of social or spiritual enlightenment—or even a benign tourist attraction—there are those who believe it to be the manifesto of a nefarious secret group of megalomaniacs bent on enslaving mankind.

In November of 2008, the collection of stones standing on a bare hill just off of Highway 77, north of Elberton, Georgia was vandalized. The slabs of Pyramid Blue granite stood nearly twenty feet tall, and had remained in this quiet pasture for twenty-eight years largely without incident. The grass was kept neatly trimmed, and the evergreen bushes that formed the border of the five-acre property were regularly pruned. It had been a peaceful, quiet piece of history nestled in the countryside of rural north Georgia.

But the peace was broken. Racial epithets and cryptic slogans were spray-painted in red across the carved faces of the megaliths. A bucket of polyepoxide was poured across several of them. The inscriptions on the stones were nearly illegible in places.

On December 15, 2008, a user calling himself "Nsane Sk8er007" uploaded a video to the popular website, YouTube.

In the video, a man describing himself as an "anonymous patriot" stood in front of the newly defaced monument in a black-hooded sweatshirt with a bandana tied around his face. Behind him, propped against the stones, were signs and posters bearing slogans that echoed the sentiments of the vandalism:

> "STOP THE NEW WORLD ORDER"
> "WE ARE NOT YOUR SLAVES"
> "NO SPP TTC NWO NAU"

The man in the video spoke in an altered voice. "This is a message to the global elite," he began.

> What you see today, at your Star Gate, the Georgia Guidestones, here in Elberton, Georgia, is but a minor fraction of what will happen if you keep meddling in our affairs. We know who you are and have only simple requests: Stop poisoning our food and water. Stop your New World Order nonsense ... Should you dare to eliminate our Constitution, our Bill of Rights, and round American citizens up with foreign troops into FEMA death camps ... patriots by the million will ascend [*sic*] on you with the ferocity of patriots that have fought before us.

He was not the first to have broadcast such a message.

To one who was unfamiliar with the whole history of

the landmark, this scene would certainly seem most bizarre. Even the most controversial of monuments in rural areas like Elberton rarely draw enough outrage to merit defacement or active protest. In the center of nearly every town in the American South there is a memorial to the Confederate dead, or a likeness of Robert E. Lee. Many who have concerns about modern-day racial inequalities have very strong feelings about these structures, but there have been no demonstrations or vandalism in their vicinity in recent years. The Georgia Guidestones, however, have always drawn a wide array of unusual attentions, despite their unassuming appearance.

The guidelines on the Guidestones only account for a portion of their renown. Only some of the controversy that surrounds Elbert County's biggest claim to fame can be linked to what is explicitly stated on the stones. Much of it is speculation and rumors of conspiracy that go far beyond northeast Georgia, and the range of opinions on the true meaning of this rural monument is very wide indeed.

The people who vandalized the stones in 2008, and the people who agree with them, profess to believe that the Georgia Guidestones are an integral part of a global plot on the part of a powerful group of unnamed individuals to subjugate and oppress the world's population and create a "New World Order." These detractors of the Guidestones have been some of the most outspoken people to discuss the subject to date. Many of them are quite active in their efforts to spread their beliefs about the stones, and some have taken those efforts even further, making public appeals to have the monument removed.

In the public forum, there are four men who have had perhaps the biggest effect on the discussion of the Guidestones within this conspiratorial context.

JIM STACHOWIAK

On November 19, 2008, *The Elberton Star* reported that the Georgia Guidestones had been heavily vandalized. Every surface of the granite monument had been spray-painted with political slogans in strong language, and the English and Swahili translations of the tenets of the Guidestones had been splashed with epoxy. The investigating authorities offered a $1,000 reward for information leading to the apprehension of the responsible party, but no arrests were ever made.

On December 15, 2008, a video was uploaded to the content-sharing website YouTube depicting a masked man standing in front of the newly defaced monument. Date-stamped the day before, the nearly five-minute-long video was entitled "A Message to the NWO from The Georgia Guidestones." The user who posted the short film to the website described it in the following words:

> An anonymous patriot appeared at the georgia guidestones, sending a riveting message to the global elite, giving them their final warning. If they do not repeal their heinous acts and restore our rights we will rise up in a way that they

> will never forget. We will overthrow every high ranking position and replace their seats with patriots while we try the elite for treason.[70]

The video begins with a brief montage of still images. The first image is of a portion of the English guides. Slowly the camera pans in until only the first tenet, "Maintain humanity under 500,000,000," is visible. An array of close-ups of individual segments of the graffiti and political signs that are propped up against the stones is shown next. Vandalism across the flagstone reads, "Stop the New World Order," while the signs further condemn a series of ideas, among them a "North American Union," the "Security and Prosperity Partnership," and the "Trans-Texas Corridor."

The camera finally settles on the image of a man in a black hooded sweatshirt. He is wearing sunglasses, and a bandana is tied around his mouth. He reads an angry message off of a piece of paper he holds in his hands. Addressing his concerns to a group of individuals that he refers to as the "Global Elite" and the "New World Order," he delivers an impassioned speech for the camera.

"Now more than ever," he says, "it is time to act. We can no longer sit by and let the malevolence of oppression work behind closed doors." He warns the "Elite" that if they proceed with the plans that he believes that they have to imprison Americans in "FEMA death camps" and to "eliminate" the United States Constitution and Bill of Rights, that "patriots" such as himself will not stand for it. "What you see before you at your Star Gate, the Georgia Guidestones," he warns, "is but a minor fraction of what will happen if you keep meddling in our affairs." He asserts that there has been an increase in American gun sales, and cautions the Elite, "You will not sleep; you will not smile."

This self-styled "Anonymous Patriot" delivered all of these proclamations under the cloak of anonymity provided by a face-mask and the voice-altering software through which he ran his words. But the mystery of the man's identity did not last for very long. A few short weeks after the original video was posted, another video appeared—this one on the Google Video website—that contained the audio recording of a phone conversation between an unknown man referred to only as "Louie" and a political activist named Jim Stachowiak.[71]

The conversation was largely about a conflict that Stachowiak was having with a woman, who in the video is simply referred to as "Patience." The source and details of that conflict are not made clear within the conversation, but in the course of the dialogue, Stachowiak says the following:

> You know what? I'm gonna go back to the Guidestones in a week. You know what I'm gonna do, Louie? I'm gonna go back and do another fucking video, and guess what I'm doing? I'm not wearing a mask. I'm gonna say—you know what? I've wore [*sic*] masks ... You know what? I'm gonna say: Fuck you, New World Order. I'm not afraid to show my face. Fuck you. Yeah, I'm the guy that was the Anonymous Patriot. Fuck you.[72]

No such second Guidestones film ever surfaced, but an Internet radio personality named Christie Aphrodite did upload a video to Google Video that included an unedited version of the "Message to the NWO" footage, wherein Stachowiak's voice was unmodified. In her video, Aphrodite also makes the claim that Stachowiak performed the vandalism as well, though she does not substantiate this allegation with any evidence.[73]

Jim Stachowiak is a complex figure in the conspiracy theory scene. On the website for his Internet talk radio show, *Freedom Fighter Radio*, he claims to have been "active in protecting, preserving, and restoring America since the age of 17 when he organized the famous Panama Canal protest."[74] Stachowiak also states that he is affiliated with the Georgia Civilian Militia, and he frequently insinuates that he is involved with the American Resistance Movement, though other members of those organizations have disputed those claims.

Stachowiak is member of a growing online community of people who describe themselves only as "Patriots." They are vehemently opposed to pieces of legislation and governmental actions that they perceive as infringements upon constitutionally protected liberties, and they seek to increase public awareness of these violations. The episodes of Stachowiak's radio show and his various self-published articles all espouse beliefs which conform to the standard platform of the Patriot movement, but some of his ideas and actions have been perceived as too radical even by his fellow Patriots.

Like many members of the movement, Stachowiak believes that the terrorist attacks on September 11, 2001, were "an inside job"[75] that the U.S. government orchestrated in order to further consolidate its power. He was a vocal opponent of the policies and procedures of George W. Bush's administration—notably the Patriot Act—but he has even more vehemently opposed himself to Barack Obama. Referring to him as "Mr. Hitler with a tan,"[76] he encourages his listeners to demand that the forty-fourth American president produce his birth certificate to prove that he is a natural-born United States citizen and therefore eligible to serve in the office he was elected to. He professes to believe that Obama and his administration are socialists and that they are linked to an elite group who seek to bring about the New World Order.

But none of those ideas are terribly controversial in Patriot circles. What has caused so many of his fellow activists to avoid him and Christie Aphrodite to develop a website that is devoted to "setting the record straight about Jim Stachowiak, his behavior and his affiliations,"[77] are his vocal expressions of dislike for certain groups and the actions that he has taken against those who disagree with him.

In December of 2008, Stachowiak was expelled from the Patriot activist group, We Are Change, for violations of that group's code of conduct. Shortly thereafter, a video was uploaded to Google Video that contained an audio recording of the conversation between Stachowiak and the local chapter head of We Are Change wherein Stachowiak was ejected from the organization. In the video, the chapter head—who seems to have been the same "Louie" to whom Stachowiak made his declaration about being the Anonymous Patriot—informs Stachowiak that he can no longer represent himself as a member of We Are Change due to his interactions with another member of the group named "Patience." Stachowiak responds to this by saying that though he is "not attacking We Are Change," he is now "going public" with his accusations against the woman named Patience. Louie states that he is going to end the call, and Stachowiak threatens, "If you end this call I'm gonna call [Child Protective Services] on Patience."[78] They argue for several minutes, and Louie finally ends the call.

A few months later, Stachowiak published an article on his website wherein he characterized We Are Change as "a front for Socialist [*sic*] who are using the youth and others to advance their Anti-American Socialist Agenda."[79]

As to whether or not Stachowiak carried through on his threat to attempt to have Patience's children removed from her custody by the authorities, reports are unclear. However, on the website for her radio show, *Truth Brigade*, Christie Aphrodite claims that Stachowiak did in fact call Child Protective Services to report allegations against herself.

Other members of the Patriot movement have also accused Stachowiak of misconduct. One individual posted a criticism of his behavior to a forum on the website *Above Top Secret* alleging that Stachowiak "was banned from Operation America Rising for statements to kill all Muslims ... [and] he was also banned from the Gathering of Eagles for fighting and nearly starting a riot at GOE1."[80]

Indeed, on at least one occasion the host of *Freedom Fighter Radio* was considered too radical by the authorities as well. On November 4, 2008, Election Day, Stachowiak was arrested outside of a polling place. Holding an American flag that was hung upside-down, and sporting a shirt printed with the words, "Kill Congress," Stachowiak stood outside the library in Evans, Georgia where voters from the area were coming to cast their ballots. He was a source of alarm for passersby, in part because he was well within the boundary past which the expression of political opinions is strictly forbidden at a polling place, but mostly because of the pepper spray, stun gun, and pistol holster that hung on his belt.

The holster, as it turned out, was empty save for a miniature reproduction of the Constitution, which, as he later asserted to a local reporter, he wore in such a fashion because "the Constitution is our best weapon against tyranny."[81] But this did not stop the Columbia County police from arresting him for disorderly conduct. According to the arresting officer, the primary cause for his detainment was not that he had violated the "no political speech" rule, but that a woman in the crowd had reported that Stachowiak told her he was a police officer. Stachowiak denied the claim, saying that he had told her the truth—which was that he was "ex-law-enforcement"[82]—and the charges were eventually dropped.

But despite the various controversies that surround him, Stachowiak has continued to record new episodes of *Freedom Fighter Radio* twice per week. He covers topics like the healthcare debates, alternative speculations on the 9/11 attacks, the tragedies at Waco and Ruby Ridge, and other common Patriot subjects. Though he has never devoted an entire show to the Georgia Guidestones, the original video of the Anonymous Patriot was posted to his blog.

From the videos and articles they have posted around the Internet, it seems clear that Stachowiak and the Patriots consider R. C. Christian's monument in Elberton to be a part of the vast global conspiracy that they call the "New World Order." What is not clear is why he made that connection in the first place. Because while Stachowiak seems to have been the "Anonymous Patriot" and may have even been the person behind the vandalism of the Guidestones, he has never specifically iterated the reasoning behind his conclusion that the monument has ties to the NWO.

But Stachowiak was not the first person to speak publicly on the matter. In fact, just one year before the stones were defaced they had appeared in the documentary *Endgame: Blueprint for Global Enslavement*, which outlined, in detail, the New World Order conspiracy theories. In the movie, the director, Alex Jones, refers to the monument briefly as "a cold testament to the Elite's sacred mission."[83] Stachowiak was certainly familiar with Jones' work—as he reposted many of the news stories from Jones' website, *Infowars*, and even devoted an entire episode of his own radio show, *Freedom Fighter Radio*, to playing back the audio component of *Endgame*—so it is quite likely that his interest in the Guidestones began with that film.

ALEX JONES

In the Patriot movement today, the work of Alex Jones is extremely influential. His nationally syndicated radio show and his websites, *Infowars* and *Prison Planet*, are mainstay sources of information on the theories and ideas espoused by the movement as a whole. While his statements on the Guidestones have been few and brief, what little he has said has likely been the only information that many people have ever heard about the monument, its meaning, and its origins.

Jones first appeared on the Patriot scene with a public access television show in Austin, Texas, wherein he would take calls from viewers live on the air. Not long thereafter, in 1996, he was brought on at a local talk radio station, KJFK, to host the show as a radio program that would come to be called *The Final Edition*. On *The Final Edition*, Jones first managed to draw national attention to himself when he orchestrated a plan to help the Branch Davidians of Waco, Texas, to rebuild the church that had been destroyed during the events of the ATF siege in 1993.[84]

Like many members of the Patriot movement, Jones' political outlook and worldview seem to have been heavily influenced by the events that transpired in the cities of Waco and Ruby Ridge in the early 1990s. In Waco, agents of the Bureau of Alcohol, Tobacco, and Firearms set out to investigate a group of people who were members of a fringe sect of the Seventh Day Adventist Church, the Branch Davidians, regarding allegations that they were in possession of illegal weaponry. But violent confrontations arose during the raid that ultimately caused the deaths of eighty civilians, twenty-five of whom were children. In Ruby Ridge, Idaho, U.S. Marshals were tasked with taking into custody a man who had failed to appear at his own trial. But the mission did not go smoothly, and in the ensuing conflict the man's wife and son were both killed.

Both events sparked massive controversy when they occurred. Among those who would become the founding members of the Patriot movement, it was perceived that in both cases, Federal authorities had overstepped their boundaries and killed innocent citizens. The federal authorities in charge of managing the siege at Waco were accused of knowingly jeopardizing the lives of the innocents inside the compound with their use of tear gas and live ammunition, and the Marshals and FBI agents at Ruby Ridge were criticized for their implementation of a non-standard set of Rules of Engagement which authorized the use of deadly force without the necessity of a verbal warning beforehand. A tide of fear and distrust of the federal government grew.

In 2000, Alex Jones directed his second feature-length documentary, *America: Wake Up (or Waco)*. In the film, Jones recounts the events of the ATF siege of the Branch Davidian compound, Mt. Carmel, in a way that is highly critical of the federal forces, referring to the raid as "government-sponsored terrorism."[85] Rejecting the official story that most of the residents of the compound died as a result of the fire that they themselves ignited—succumbing to wounds received both from both the flames and the detonation of ammunition that the Branch Davidians had stockpiled inside—Jones claims that the videos of the siege that were released were doctored to support the government "cover-up," and that federal agents were directly responsible for the deaths. At several points in the film, he calls for indictments of the federal officials responsible for the raid, especially Attorney General Janet Reno, who he refers to as "Hermann Göring in drag."[86]

By contrast, Jones portrays the Branch Davidians in a very sympathetic light, interviewing the grieving mother of their leader, David Koresh, and highlighting the number of children who died during the siege. "No matter what propaganda you want to believe," Jones states, "those babies did not deserve to be murdered by the black ski-mask thugs."[87]

The tone of the film as a whole is decidedly hostile and untrusting of the United States government, and Jones makes frequent reference to other theories of federal malfeasance—the alleged smuggling of Nazi scientists into the country after WWII and the staging of the Oklahoma City bombing, among others—all of which feed into the grander conspiracy theory that is propagated by the Patriot movement. "Welcome to the New World Order," Jones says angrily as he stands over the wrecked remains of the Mt. Carmel compound. Because he, like many other Patriots, does not believe that the siege in Waco, Texas, was an isolated incident. They believe that it was but a small part of a vast global conspiracy that has been at work in the world for centuries.

In 2007, Alex Jones made a film that attempts to explain the totality of that conspiracy. The documentary, *Endgame: Blueprint for Global Destruction* is Jones' most successful and popular film to date. In it, he outlines the evidence as he sees it that a group of people in positions of power, referred to interchangeably as the "Power Elite" and the "Global Elite," have been manipulating political systems and world events in order to bring about a state referred to as the "New World Order."

At the beginning of the film, Jones posits an Orwellian

possible future that he believes will occur if the "Elite" are able to successfully execute their plans:

> In the near future, Earth is dominated by a powerful world government. Once-free nations are slaves to the will of a tiny Elite. The dawn of a new Dark Age is upon mankind. Countries are a thing of the past. Every form of independence is under attack, with the family, and even the individual itself, nearing extinction. Close to eighty percent of the Earth's population has been eliminated. The remnants of a once-free humanity are forced to live within highly controlled, compact, prison-like cities ... No human activity is private: AI supercomputers chronicle and categorize every action. A prison planet dominated by a ruthless gang of control-freaks whose power can never be challenged: this is the vision of the Global Elite, their goal ... A worldwide control grid, designed to ensure the overlords' monopoly of power forever. Our species will be condemned to this nightmare future unless the masses are awakened to the New World Order master plan and mobilized to defeat it.[88]

There are a wide variety of theories as to what the exact goals and plans for the New World Order are, but Jones explains the most prevalent ones in *Endgame*. The most unifying of these theories is that the "Elite" are attempting to create a single world government and to abolish the concept of nationhood. Proponents of this theory see the Guidestones as "a testament to the Elite's plan for a world religion, global laws with a global court and army to enforce it [*sic*]"[89] because they advocate the institution of a world court in the sixth tenet, "Let all nations rule internally, resolving external disputes in a world court." NWO believers see the creation of both the United Nations and the European Union as frightening harbingers of a plan nearing fruition.

Rumors that the United States, Mexico, and Canada are planning to join together, politically and economically, into a North American Union styled after the European Union are indicative of these fears. As evidence of the United States' willingness to join such a coalition, Jones cites the planning of the Trans-Texas Corridor—a transportation network that was proposed in 2005 as a way of routing the high volume of long-distance freight and traffic from Mexico around major population centers. Patriot critics of the TTC saw it as a method of strengthening U.S. ties to Mexico, both physically and symbolically. In 2009, the project was officially discontinued due to extreme public outcry.

Jones and his supporters believe that the NAU would just be the next step on the way to a single world government. Once North America was united, a similar alliance would occur in Asia, and then the two mega-nations, along with the EU, would merge to become one global power.

Another very common theme within New World Order conspiracy theories is eugenics. First codified in 1865 by

Sir Francis Galton, eugenics is the practice of guided evolution and genetic modification of human beings. It could theoretically allow a society to institute a breeding program to intentionally increase the frequency of the physical and mental characteristics that it considered desirable in mankind and decrease the frequency of those deemed undesirable. In the late nineteenth and early twentieth centuries, the idea of eugenics was quite popular among scientists and statesmen alike. But after Adolf Hitler put into practice some of the theories of eugenics during his reign in Germany—attempting to use them to "purify" the "Aryan race"—the prevailing public sentiment for the so-called science turned sour.

Alex Jones suggests, however, that the application of eugenics in Western countries neither began nor ended with the Third Reich. He states that oil magnate John Rockefeller exported concepts of eugenics to Germany and that the ideas of eugenics and social Darwinism did not in fact fall out of fashion but merely rebranded themselves as the modern ideas of "trans-humanism, population control, sustainability, conservation, and environmentalism."[90] Jones also asserts that Nazi eugenicists were smuggled into the Allied nations to continue their work after the end of WWII. Citing as evidence the compulsory sterilization laws that existed in thirty-one U.S. states until the late 1970s—under which authority thousands of patients in mental institutions were forcibly removed of their ability to reproduce—Jones insinuates that the program of eugenics still continues to this day in America. "The Elite have left a massive wave of destruction behind them," Jones says, "as they cold-bloodedly experiment on civilian populations as if we are [*sic*] lab rats."[91]

Adherents of the NWO theory also believe that the "Elite" are working to eradicate roughly eighty percent of the world's population. In the minds of these supporters this is further evidence that the Georgia Guidestones are part of the Elite's plot because "set in stone it is written that the population never rise above five-hundred million."[92] Jones argues that population control will begin as a global one-child policy like the one currently in place in China. He implicates celebrities such as Bill and Melinda Gates, Ted Turner and Warren Buffett as being part of the conspiracy because of their major contributions to organizations devoted to reducing over-population.

But he does not believe that population reduction will be limited to restrictions on breeding. In discussing the controversial claims of some scientists that an outbreak of a virus like Ebola would be beneficial to the human race because it would drastically reduce its numbers, Jones ominously portends more dire measures that the "Elite" might take. He claims that the "dark builders" plan to intentionally release bio-weapons on the population at large, disguising this dispersal as a terrorist attack.

To the Patriots, perhaps the most damning piece of evidence against the Georgia Guidestones is that they were "erected by a secretive group."[93] Those who subscribe to the theories about the NWO contend that its agenda is being pushed by a small group of the "Global Elite," men and women in possession of great amounts both of power and wealth. Jones asserts that this group evolved out of secret societies of the early Renaissance like the Freemasons and the Rosicrucians. The members, he contends, worked in secret because their agenda was to subvert national governments and the Church. And he believes that members of similar societies today work to do exactly the same thing.

In July of 2000, Alex Jones set out to infiltrate a private men's club called the Bohemian Club at their notorious retreat at Bohemian Grove in northern California. In recent years, the Bohemian Club has been the subject of much speculation by conspiracy theorists, mostly as a result of its having so many high-profile members. Despite being founded as a society primarily for artists, its membership today in large part consists of the CEOs of large corporations, the heads of financial institutions and defense contract companies, and even some U.S. presidents. At their annual retreat in Bohemian Grove, the membership is frequently supplemented by foreign dignitaries who are invited as guests of the active members.

Alex Jones made a documentary film, *Dark Secrets Inside Bohemian Grove*, about his activities infiltrating the group, and British journalist Jon Ronson featured Jones and his exploits at the retreat in a four-part investigative television series, *Secret Rulers of the World*. Jones recorded footage of his experiences in the Grove, notably the "Cremation of Care" ceremony, with a hidden camera on his companion's belt, and provided analysis of that footage in his documentary.

The footage shows Jones and a friend entering the rustic, wooded campground that is Bohemian Grove through a break in the forest that surrounds it. In *Dark Secrets*, Jones claims that he was stopped numerous times by the security personnel—not only men from the local sheriff's department, but also the Secret Service—but these confrontations do not appear on the tape, a fact that Jones explains by claiming that they did not have enough digital storage on the camera to record the entirety of their exploration. Most of the video is, in fact, unquestionably innocuous, revealing only quaintly primitive living, cooking, and dining quarters and drunken middle-aged campers chatting and singing along to old rock-and-roll songs while an off-camera musician plays the bagpipes in the distance. But there are plenty of things that Jones does find sinister throughout the camp.

He comments on the frequency with which he sees signs written in Latin and French, and takes fastidious care to document each stone owl—the symbol of the Bohemian Club—that they find in the Grove. But the real threat that Alex perceives is in the famed "Cremation of Care" ceremony, a kind of pageant performed on the first night of the retreat every year.

In Jones' footage of the ceremony, a large crowd of onlookers is shown watching as the robed actors process onto the staging area across the lake as bagpipes play. The procession itself is made invisible to the camera by the darkness, but Jones claims that he saw cloaked men walking before a carriage and carrying a "bound body."[94] Then the procession reaches the better-illuminated center of the stage, and the main actor in the pageant recites several poetically worded lines extolling the virtues and beauty of the natural environment around them. He then enjoins them to "shake off [their] sorrows with the city's dust and cast to the winds the cares of life."[95]

Then the music swells, and the meat of the ceremony begins. The lead actor announces, "By the power of your fellowship, Dull Care is slain,"[96] and the audience cheers. He explains that the bundle is Care's body, which has been brought to the "funeral pyre," and a man in a boat ferries the "corpse" across the lake to the prepared fire pit. Then the voice of Care taunts them, saying that though they burn him every year in the Grove, he is always waiting when they return to the "marketplace." The lead actor counters this, saying that though Care has power over them throughout the rest of the year, they are able to banish him for at least the space of their holiday. They continue back and forth for a time, until finally the fire is ignited and the bundle with it.

Alex Jones explains his interpretation of this ceremony in his documentary. He sees it as a pagan rite developed to worship the ancient god, Moloch, by simulating a human sacrifice. As evidence of this he cites the cover of the program that he was given as a member of the audience that night. On the cover of the program—which reads "Cremation of Care 2000, Directed by Craig Jones"—there is a picture of the central area of the stage during the ritual. A figure stands in front of a large fire. Jones "enhances" the picture and claims he sees a figure in the flames that "anatomical experts"[97] whom he consulted agree can only be that of a human baby. At one point in the documentary, Jones also claims that in addition to the symbolic "Cremation of Care," there may also be an actual human sacrifice performed at Bohemian Grove, "according to some occult experts,"[98] but he does not elaborate on or cite his sources for this allegation.

Jones believes that the Bohemian Grove retreat is further evidence that there is an underhanded conspiracy between members of a "Global Elite," but others who have witnessed the events there have expressed differing opinions. Journalist Jon Ronson commented in his own documentary that it seemed like the members there were just "sacrificing all their troubles in the world for a two-week holiday,"[99] not miming a pagan child sacrifice. Ronson also would also later say that his "lasting impression [of the Grove] was of an all-pervading sense of immaturity: the Elvis impersonators, the pseudo-pagan spooky rituals, the heavy drinking. These people might have reached the apex of their professions but emotionally they seemed trapped in their college years."[100]

But whatever the true meaning of the "Cremation of Care" ceremony, to Alex Jones and other Patriots like him, the pageant is most terrifying because of its seemingly "pagan" trappings. Because while it is generally not overly emphasized in Jones' work in particular, another of the common elements in the New World Order theories is that the conspiratorial plot of the "Global Elite" is satanic, pagan, or anti-Christian in nature.

MARK DICE

In July of 2005, Alex Jones interviewed a guest on his radio show who spoke under the pseudonym "John Conner." As a fellow subscriber to the New World Order conspiracy theory, Jones asked Conner to summarize his opinions on the subject.

Conner explained that while he agreed with everything that Jones had said about the matter, to him the New World Order seemed to have an additional dimension to it. The master plan of the "Elite," he insisted is "not only a political venture ...but it is a spiritual venture."[101] To explain, he went on to say, "the president of the New World Order will one day be the Antichrist, and that's what this is all leading up to."[102]

Many Christians today believe that the final book of the New Testament, Revelation is a literal and prophetic account of how the world will one day end. In this futurist Christian eschatology, it is believed that a variety of globally catastrophic events will occur that will ultimately lead to the end of life on Earth, God's vanquishing of Satan, and a final judgment whereby God assesses the merits of all of the souls that ever were, damning some and rewarding the others. A key component in this narrative is the figure of the "Antichrist." It is believed by those who subscribe to this theory of the "end times" that a man will come to rule the Earth while the plagues and catastrophes are visiting mankind, and that he will be seen by many to be the Second Coming of Jesus Christ, but in fact he will be just the opposite. This man will lead the people further away from the path of God through his deceit, which will only cause God to wreak further havoc on the world.

A subset of the Patriot population believes that this eschatological prophecy and the New World Order conspiracy are intrinsically linked. Among these, Mark Dice—or "John Conner," as he called himself until 2007—is perhaps the most vocal public figure. The New World Order, Dice claims, is "a satanic plan to give birth to the Antichrist."[103] He believes that the evil figure discussed in Revelation is a member of the "Global Elite," and that the Elite themselves are attempting to control the world, not only for the money and power, but also to further the agenda of the devil. "They are fulfilling Bible prophecy," he asserts.[104]

Mark Dice first gained mainstream notoriety in 2005, when he asserted publicly that pop star Jessica Simpson was "a singing stripper" after seeing one of her music videos.[105] He branded the starlet as a bad role model, and cited her as just another example of the corruption of Christian values in America today. The attention that this comment brought him allowed him to secure guest spots on Patriot radio programs like *The Alex Jones Show* to spread the totality of his message. And one of Dice's favored topics of discussion, both in these guest appearances and in his own books, is the Georgia Guidestones.

Like Alex Jones and Jim Stachowiak, Mark Dice firmly believes that the Georgia Guidestones were created as a symbol of the New World Order. But Dice takes this a step further, saying that the stones "have a deep satanic origin and message."[106] He asserts that the stones were erected by a secret society of the Global Elite that he calls the "Illuminati," and he considers the monument to be "empirical evidence of the Illuminati's agenda."[107] Because of these beliefs, he and the group he founded, The Resistance, issued a press release in the summer of 2008 calling for the removal and destruction of the stones:

> We have atheists and Satanists getting the Bible's ten commandments removed from pub-

> lic property, yet the satanic Georgia Guidestones have stood for decades, and nobody seems to care. Well, we do.[108]

Dice's dislike for the monument is founded partially on its resemblance to Stonehenge, a historically pagan site, but it is predominantly based on the tenets that are engraved in the granite, which he calls "the Illuminati's ten commandments, a mockery of the Christian Ten Commandments."[109] He objects strongly to the messages that he perceives are encoded in the words of the precepts.

The first and second tenets of the Guidestones—"Maintain population under 500,000,000 in perpetual balance with nature" and "Guide reproduction wisely – improving fitness and diversity," respectively—are for Dice, as for many Patriots, the most indicative that the monument is linked to the New World Order. Conspiracy theorists have long proposed that a large part of the Elite's plan involves the elimination of a large portion of the population because "all the work has been done" in creating the infrastructure for the NWO, and now all of the "useless eaters"[110] are no longer necessary to them. Dice sees these two tenets as supportive of that plan, as they propose a population cap that is much smaller than the current world population, and "obviously guiding reproduction means … forced sterilization,"[111] another common trend in NWO conspiracies.

The third precept, "Unite humanity with a living new language," Dice finds objectionable largely due to his Christian perspective. It conjures to his mind the story of Babel, the biblical city where all men spoke a common language, until God intentionally confused them into speaking many tongues. Some biblical scholars have argued that the people of Babel were confounded because of their hubris, and thus many Christians believe that a globally common language would be an affront to God. Similarly, the words of the fourth guide, "Rule passion – faith – tradition – and all things with tempered reason," evoke the idea of religious intolerance to Dice. "This of course is suggesting judicial control over matters of faith and religion,"[112] he says, claiming that one day "Christianity will be deemed a heresy"[113] and forbidden by the "Elite."

In the fifth suggestion that the Guidestones make to "Protect people and nations with fair laws and just courts," Dice takes issue with the vagueness of the wording. He worries who will decide "what is 'fair' and what is 'just,'"[114] and he rejects the implication that it is the job of the government to protect the people. His complaints are much the same for the seventh tenet—"Eliminate petty laws and useless officials"—saying that while, on the surface, this sounds reasonable, it is actually a way of saying that the Illuminati are going to "streamline the legal code lending all power of interpretation to the individuals who hold the power."[115]

A further red flag is raised for Dice in the sixth precept, which enjoins mankind to "Let all nations rule internally, resolving external disputes in a world court." Despite the mention here of separate national rule, to the Patriots who fear the coming of the New World Order, the establishment of a world court is just a step in the direction of the establishment of a unified world government. Dice calls this injunction "chilling" and claims that it suggests "the New World Order's world court should oversee all matters."[116]

Dice admits that the last three guidelines seem "fairly benign,"[117] but he holds that this is only true on the surface. "We have to be very careful with the semantics ... and the interpretations of these commandments,"[118] he says. He suggests that it takes a careful reading to be able to decode the Illuminati messages within the stones. In the eighth tenet, for example, he asserts that the suggestion to "Balance personal rights with social duties" is actually a "socialist" mandate that portends that individuals will be required to sacrifice their rights under the New World Order. The ninth dictate to "Prize truth – beauty – love – seeking harmony with the infinite," while seeming merely poetic to the layman, speaks of Satanism to Mark Dice. "Who is the Infinite?" he asks. "We know the Infinite to the Illuminati is Lucifer."[119] And in the final lines of the inscription, "Be not a cancer on the Earth – Leave room for nature – Leave room for nature," Dice perceives an insult to humanity. He states that this is the Illuminati asserting, "the vast population of planet Earth has become a consuming cancer,"[120] further justification for the planned massive depopulation that he feels is alluded to in the very first guide.

The mystery of the true identity of R. C. Christian and the group that he claims to represent is also very unsettling to Mark Dice. He holds that all secret societies are diabolical in nature, stating that the only possible reason for their secrecy is that "if people knew they were worshipping Satan, they would freak out."[121] Like Alex Jones, he believes that the "Elite" originated in the secret societies of the early Renaissance, but Dice goes on to say that they have kept alive the "satanic ideologies,"[122] passing them down through time to further the aims of the devil.

The Georgia Guidestones, Dice asserts, were not just built by any secret society either, but by one of the ones that he considers to be the worst. Like many who believe that the Guidestones hold a positive message, Dice believes that the creator of the stones was a Rosicrucian, but to him this is not a good thing. He feels that the pseudonym, "R. C. Christian" clearly "stands for an individual representing the Order of the Rose Cross," which he describes as a "perverted occult sect of Christianity."[123]

He brands the Rosicrucians as among the more dangerous secret societies because their beliefs and values are too similar to those of Christianity. Similar though these teachings are, Dice feels that they are nevertheless incorrect. "The distortions and errors are clear to those who know the Word," he says, "but only serve to deceive Rosicrucians and draw them from the Truth."[124] Many Christians who take a literal view of the eschatology in the Bible are wary of things that approximate Christian teachings but are not exactly right, because of the predictions in the Bible that there will be many false prophets who pretend to be godly but are not.

Dice's judgment that R. C. Christian must have been a Rosicrucian is, for him, really the only thing he needs in order to decide that the Georgia Guidestones are affiliated with the New World Order. For he believe that it is the mission of Mormons, Freemasons, Satanists, and Rosicrucians "to dissolve True Christianity into the world religion of the New World Order, so the Antichrist can declare that he is the savior of humanity, and King of the Earth."[125]

While Mark Dice was once the most vocal public detractor of the Guidestones to be found, for several years now he has been relatively silent on the subject. Others have taken up the cause, however, and one man in particular has added a few new dimensions to the theory that the monument is deeply connected with the New World Order conspiracy.

VAN SMITH

Despite being a bit of a latecomer to the conspiracy theory scene, Arkansas native Van Smith has made quite a few contributions to the theories surrounding the Georgia Guidestones. Unlike many of the people who have spoken out about the monument, Smith does not consider himself to be a Patriot activist, or indeed an activist of any kind. A self-described "ordinary man,"[126] he makes his living with a computer business and only became interested in the Guidestones after helping his children, who are homeschooled, to complete a scholastic project about them. So disinterested is he in the general realm of conspiracy theories that he refers to the Guidestones as an "unwelcome distraction"[127] from his work. But he claims that he has continued to post his research on his website, *Van's Hardware Journal*, "despite the potential risks to [his] career and growing business because the stakes involved for humanity are so grave."[128]

In common with men like Alex Jones and Mark Dice, Smith believes that the Georgia Guidestones are part of an Illuminati plot to bring about the New World Order. But Smith's reason for believing that the Elbert County landmark is connected to a nefarious global conspiracy is very different. Whereas most Patriots connect the two based on perceived similarities between the values espoused on the stones and the values that they presume the "Elite" to hold, Smith believes that there is a more tangible link, and the key to it lies in the Burj Khalifa.

The Burj Khalifa—or Burj Dubai, as it was known during its construction—is an enormous skyscraper in the United Arab Emirates. Located in the heart of the most populous city in the UAE, Dubai, the Burj is currently the tallest man-made structure ever built, and for some this is cause for alarm. Since construction on the building began in 2004, some fringe members of the Christian population in the United States, including Van Smith, have speculated that the aim of the Burj's creators is to build a "new Tower of Babel."[129]

In the book of Genesis, a story is told about an ancient city that would come to be called Babel. It states that following a great flood that wiped out nearly all life on Earth, all of the remaining people were gathered together in one place, and they all spoke one common language. These people decided to build a large city with an extravagantly tall tower in the center of it. But in the tale, God sees what the people are doing and becomes upset, saying:

> Behold, the people is one, and they have all one language; and this they begin to do: and now nothing will be restrained from them, which they have imagined to do. Go to, let us go down, and there confound their language, that they may not understand one another's speech. (Genesis 11:6–7 KJV)

He then destroys the city and scatters the people, causing them to speak in many languages instead of one. As with most biblical passages, a variety of interpretations of this story have been proposed by different individuals, but the meaning that Smith takes away from the passage is that the building of a tower so tall was an affront to God.

And Smith sees the Burj Khalifa in a similar light. To him, the erection of another extraordinarily tall tower—nearly one thousand feet taller than the CN Tower in Toronto, which held the record for the tallest freestanding building before the Burj—must be related in some way to the story of the Tower of Babel. "The symbolic meaning of the Burj Khalifa is unambiguous," he writes. "It is the completion of the second Tower of Babel, a pursuit the Rosicrucians, Freemasons, and their ilk have sought for millennia."[130]

The connection that Van Smith sees between the Burj Khalifa and the Georgia Guidestones is less immediately clear, however. While the Burj stands at a remarkable 828 meters tall, the Guidestones have an overall height of merely 5.87 meters, and the circumstances surrounding the creation of the two structures seem utterly dissimilar. Nevertheless, Smith asserts that the connection is "virtually a mathematical certainty."[131] As the basis for this claim, Smith discloses a series of numerological calculations that he has made with the physical dimensions of the Georgia Guidestones.

To begin with, he assesses the measurements of the capstone, the central Gnomon stone, and each of the major stones. The capstone, he observes, is—rounding all measurements to the nearest meter—three meters long, two meters wide, and half a meter thick, meaning that its proportions are 6:4:1. Rounding again, the Gnomon stone is five meters high, one meter wide, and half a meter thick, which gives it a proportional value of 10:2:1. Finally, each of the four major stones is approximately five meters high, two meters wide, and half a meter thick by Smith's calculations, yielding a ratio of 10:4:1.

By rearranging the numbers in the proportional value of each of the major stones, Smith comes up with the numbers one, four, and ten, which he then chooses to interpret as a date: January 4, 2010. He points out that this is the day that the Burj Khalifa was first opened to the public. Similarly, he rearranges the numbers in the proportions of the capstone to yield one, four, and six and interprets this as a date as well: January 4, 2006. This, Smith highlights, is the day that the former prime minister of the UAE and emir of Dubai, Maktoum bin Rashad Al Maktoum, died following a heart attack.

For a final calculation, Smith sums the numbers in the proportion of the capstone—one, four, and six—to get eleven; then he adds together the numbers of the proportion of the

Gnomon stone—one, two, and ten—to get thirteen. He then sums the proportion of the each of the major stones—one, four, and ten—which yields the number fifteen, but he adds the number four to this as well, as there are four of the major stones, and comes up with the number nineteen. Finally, he takes the three numbers that he derived in this fashion—eleven, thirteen, and nineteen—and multiplies them together. The number this produces is 2,717, which Smith notes is the exact height, in feet, of the Burj Khalifa.

Van Smith considers the above numerical connections between the Georgia Guidestones and the Burj Khalifa to be "so solid that they are virtually indisputable,"[132] and it is for this reason that he is convinced of the monument's association with the New World Order. All of Smith's self-described "incontrovertible evidence"[133] is based upon a numerology of his own devising, but he asserts that this is appropriate as, given the frequent application of numerology among theosophists, he finds it quite likely that R. C. Christian intentionally encoded "numerological messages"[134] into the structure of the Guidestones. Smith, like Mark Dice, maintains a strong belief that the monument's anonymous founder was himself representative of an occult group, and Smith asserts that it was likely a theosophical one.

"It is immediately evident," he claims, "to even the most casual observer possessing only rudimentary understanding of modern occult beliefs that the Georgia Guidestones is the product of theosophy."[135] Van Smith's understanding of theosophy seems somewhat limited given his assertion that it is a "term that encompasses the Freemasons [and] Rosicrucians,"[136] two groups whose origins predate the development of theosophical doctrine by centuries, but he freely admits that he is no expert on the occult and secret societies in general, and that he is only interested in them at all due to their apparent connections with the Guidestones. But from the knowledge that he does have, he has come to the same conclusion that many other conspiracy theorists have reached—that theosophy and all other occult philosophies are abhorrent:

> The body of occult work in active use today is like an endless, sticky, black ocean of tar. I have had the misfortune of swimming in that sea of engulfing darkness while researching this article. For an analytical, reasoning mind, the occult is offensive. For the moral, the occult topics relevant for this article are shocking and repulsive.[137]

The central tenet of theosophy is that all religions are attempts by mankind to perfect its own nature and to achieve a higher, more enlightened state. Smith believes that by this, theosophists mean that they are attempting to make themselves into gods who will preside above the rest of humanity in the coming New World Order. And he sees the latest skyscraper in Dubai as symbolic of that attempt. "The Burj Khalifa not only signifies a supreme Luciferian attempt to defy and defeat God," he asserts, "but the completion of the Tower is, for them the beginning of a new age where man can become like God."[138] The Georgia Guidestones are then implicated in this plan as well, he feels, not only due to the content of the words etched into them, but also because of their numerological association with the Burj.

Van Smith also has a few relatively unique ideas about the potential identity of R. C. Christian. He posits first and foremost that he does not believe that the pseudonym was only used by one person, asserting that the author of *Common Sense Renewed* and the man who actually went to Elberton to commission the Guidestones are two separate people. He does not further substantiate this claim, however. He also writes that he believes that Atlanta media mogul Ted Turner was at least a member of the group that Christian claimed to represent. This he claims is proved by Turner's frequent public assertion that the United States should mandate a one-child limit on families, as is practiced in China, and also by the fact that Wyatt Martin was reported to have known him. Perhaps most interestingly, Smith hypothesizes that R. C. Christian may be the subject of a relief sculpture that is in Elberton, Georgia. The sculpture was commissioned to be a bust of Franklin Roosevelt, and it is labeled as such to this day, but Smith asserts that it "looks nothing like"[139] the United States president and is therefore suspect.

There are a wide variety of opinions as to the meaning and origin of the Georgia Guidestones, and Smith does take the time to address his take on one that is opposed to his own. He finds the theory that the Guidestones were built to help the survivors of a nuclear holocaust or other disaster to rebuild society far-fetched due to the "decidedly unbenevolent [*sic*] attitude of Luciferian cultists,"[140] who he believes designed the monument. He further states that there is "no reputable scientific evidence" to support that theory, whereas "there are good reasons to believe that the Georgia Guidestones is an arrogant advertisement for the demented plans of a deranged but powerful cult to overthrow national governments and install a totalitarian global government."[141]

Through his website and the interviews that he has given in the past few years, Van Smith has made quite clear his own opinions about the "abomination to humanity"[142] that he considers the Georgia Guidestones to be. But like most of the conspiracy theorists who have studied the monument, he has only given the most cursory of attentions to the book written by its founder to explain it. Further study of *Common Sense Renewed* and the scant details that are known of R. C. Christian himself provide a very different perspective on the meaning and purpose of the mysterious collection of granite stones.

11. Workers at the Elberton Granite Finishing Company preparing one of the four main stones

12. Stonecutter Charlie Clamp sandblasting the text of the English-language face of the Guidestones

CHAPTER 5:

THE MAN BEHIND THE MONUMENT

Much of the controversy that surrounds the Georgia Guidestones is centered around the speculations of various groups with regards to the authorial intent of the monument. Everyone familiar with the structure seems to have an opinion as to why its mysteriously anonymous creator commissioned it. This, however, is one question that is not left completely unanswered by R. C. Christian. The entire second chapter of Christian's treatise, *Common Sense Renewed*, is devoted to answering it.

In that chapter Christian clearly enumerates the motivations that he claims caused him to take this particular action. Throughout the course of the remainder of the book, he outlines all of the political and social beliefs that he holds that give context to those motivations. Assuming that he did not deliberately dissemble to create a false impression of himself, this text uniquely resolves the matter of Christian's purpose in erecting the Guidestones.

In "The Georgia Guidestones," the second chapter of his book, Christian asserts the following:

> I am the originator of the Georgia Guidestones and the sole author of its inscriptions. I have had the assistance of a number of other American citizens in bringing the monument

> into being. We have no mysterious purpose or ulterior motives. We seek common sense pathways to a peaceful world, without bias for particular creeds or philosophies ... Stonehenge and other vestiges of ancient thought arouse our curiosity but carry no message for human guidance. The Guidestones have been erected to convey certain ideas across time to others. We hope that these silent stones and their inscriptions will merit a degree of approval and acceptance down the centuries, and by their silent persistence hasten in small ways the dawning of an age of reason.[143]

Explicitly, then, Christian's purpose in commissioning the Georgia Guidestones was to promote a peaceful, sustainable society throughout the ages. He sought to do this by leaving behind a message, in the form of the ten precepts that are etched into the monument.

Those particular precepts, however, have been a source of contention throughout the whole of the Guidestones' existence. They were phrased concisely so as to conform to the restrictions of space on the structure itself, but that same brevity makes them somewhat vague and open to a variety of interpretations. In *Common Sense Renewed*, Christian outlined his beliefs and ideas at greater length, thereby providing a much-needed tool for the understanding of Christian's intentions.

The mystery of Robert Christian's true identity has remained unsolved for thirty years. Wyatt Martin, the only man known to have the answer to the mystery, has kept his silence. Many people have put forth their speculations about the matter, but no hard evidence has ever emerged to implicate one particular individual. That said, careful as he was, Christian did leave some clues in his wake. They may never lead to a discovery of the enigmatic man's real name, but they can help to engender an understanding of the sort of person that he was.

THE LIFE OF ROBERT CHRISTIAN

Only three people are known to have actually met the man who called himself "R. C. Christian" in person. He first introduced himself to the president of the Elberton Granite Finishing Company in 1979, Joe Fendley. From there, he made contact with the man who would become both his financial intermediary and something of a friend, Wyatt Martin, then president of the Granite City Bank. Joe Fendley has since passed away, and Wyatt Martin is now over eighty years old and in failing health. But Fendley also introduced Mr. Christian to another member of the Elberton Community, EGA member Hudson Cone. Fendley and Martin both recorded recollections of their encounters with the mysterious man in various places before it became too late for them to share what they knew with the world, and Cone remains alive and well enough to tell his part of the story. Only from these accounts is it possible to gain any knowledge of Christian's appearance and demeanor.

In a pamphlet he published shortly after the monument was completed, Joe Fendley described the man who walked into his office to commission the Georgia Guidestones as simply "middle-aged" and "neatly dressed."[144] Financial intermediary Wyatt Martin was able to provide a little more detail, recalling that he was "probably about 5'11". He had on a normal business suit with a tie. He wore a hat."[145] Martin also observed that he was "well-spoken, obviously an educated person."[146] In his own book, *Common Sense Renewed*, Robert Christian mentions that "for more than 60 years [he has] benefitted from the American political system."[147] From this last it can be reasonably extrapolated that at the time of the book's first printing in 1986, the man was already more than sixty years old.

Hudson Cone's recollections of Christian corroborate this. By his estimation, the strange man was in his "early seventies" when he met him. Cone laments the fact that he had only a brief and "hurried conversation" with Christian, but he did get a very good look at the man. He agreed that Christian was tall—though his own estimate was that he stood about "6'2" or 6'3"." He noted also that he was quite thin, "not gaunt looking, but certainly thin," and "bald-headed." When he spoke, he had a midwestern American accent, as well. "I've been hunting up in Iowa," Cone muses, "and I would say that he would definitely be from Iowa according to his accent." If this is true, then it might explain why Christian chose a small Iowa publisher to produce his book. These little clues paint a physical portrait that is imperfect at best, but they do at least add to the greater sketch of Christian's character.

About the life of the man, a little more can be determined. Christian was demonstrably a man of at least some means. Though Wyatt Martin has never chosen to reveal the exact sum of money that was paid out to Joe Fendley and his extensive crew for their labor and the cost of the granite, he has made it clear that it was substantial. And Fendley, when presented with the rumor that the figure was "in the neighborhood of fifty thousand dollars … said that that estimate was much too low."[148] In Fendley's own recollections about the day he met Christian, he stated that he initially quoted the stranger an approximate price that was so high, he expected the man to balk then and there. No monument the size of the Georgia Guidestones had ever been created in Elbert County before, and special equipment had to be devised and implemented solely for the project. The price of such an undertaking was undoubtedly relatively high, and even if Christian did, as he said, have "the assistance of a number of other American citizens in bringing the monument into being,"[149] a significant portion of the funds to support the project would likely have come from his own assets.

But his means were not unlimited. Hudson Cone recalls that Christian spoke at length about the outer ring of stones that were never placed around the Guidestones, which he referred to as the "moon stones." Evidently, Christian and his organization had "run out of money" for that portion of the project, and at the time that Cone was speaking to him—shortly after the unveiling of the monument—they were actively petitioning environmentally-oriented nonprofit organizations to see if they could provide the funds. But as there remain no slabs of granite around the monument to mark the progression of the moon throughout the month, this attempt was apparently unsuccessful.

In March of 2010, it was revealed that Christian had a son. Wyatt Martin spoke to a journalist from CNN and informed him that he had been contacted by the son of R. C. Christian, who gave him the news that the mystery man had passed on.[150] Martin has since commented that, while most people would not recognize the real name of Mr. Christian, "his son was probably a more notable, known person than he was."[151]

We can also surmise that Christian traveled frequently and to diverse locations. Wyatt Martin, who was the only person with whom the mysterious man would communicate after his initial visits to Elberton, indicated in an interview with *Wired* magazine that "all of Mr. Christian's correspondence came from different cities around the country. He never sent anything from the same place twice."[152] The financier also indicated that many of the places Christian visited were undeveloped and impoverished nations, such as Bangladesh. Martin felt that the man's experiences in these countries had certainly contributed to his motivations in planning the Guidestones project, because such an educated man would have felt compelled to try to help resolve the issues that created so much human suffering.[153]

Wyatt Martin's impression with regards to Christian's level of education is supported by other evidence. The very structure of the Georgia Guidestones, which was very specifically mandated by Christian, tends to imply a broad range of experience in its author. The astrological features are strongly reminiscent of the historical British site of Stonehenge, a fact which Christian himself admitted to Martin was no coincidence. Christian told the banker that he had traveled to many famous landmarks, but that he was especially affected by his visit to Stonehenge. Reportedly, he also recited Henry James' lines about the ancient monument to Martin: "You may put a hundred questions to these rough hewn giants as they bend in grim contemplation of their fallen companions; but your curiosity falls dead in the vast sunny stillness that enshrouds them."[154]

James was not the only writer with whom Christian displayed a familiarity. The title of his own book is an allusion to Thomas Paine's influential political treatise, *Common Sense*, and indeed the first chapter of *Common Sense Renewed* opens with a brief description of Paine's life and ideas. Throughout the course of the book he also makes reference to the ideas of Gregor Mendel, Mark Twain, Isaac Newton, Charles Darwin, Albert Einstein, Karl Marx, Blaise Pascal, Galileo, and Socrates.

But even this evidence of his cultural literacy pales in comparison to the indication in his writings of his worldly awareness. He writes at length about the American political and economic systems, noting both their historical developments and their modern circumstances, but he does not confine himself to the discussion of domestic institutions alone. He also exhibits a remarkable knowledge of the governments and societies of several other nations, among them Russia, Japan, Sweden and China, referring to them frequently with both positive and negative comparisons to the United States.

Hudson Cone saw further evidence of the mysterious benefactor's level of education, in his seemingly high degree of knowledge about plant-life. Cone hypothesized that the man may have been "some sort of naturalist" because during their conversation he frequently "called trees by their botanical names." Christian also told Cone that he had recently visited the Joyce Kilmer Memorial Forest near Robbinsville, North Carolina, to "see a certain kind of tree that grows up there and nowhere else." If Christian was a botanist, or even simply a botanical enthusiast, that could account for the strong message of conservationism that is conveyed by the Guidestones.

Christian reveals another detail about himself in *Common Sense Renewed*. He discloses that some of his ancestors fought in the Revolutionary War, and that others fought on both sides of the American Civil War. According to Wyatt Martin, Christian himself had also been a military man for at least a time, as he served as a fighter pilot in World War II. If he was a career soldier and perhaps still a member of the armed forces when he commissioned the Guidestones in 1979, then this could be one potential explanation for his many travels.

All precise ideas regarding who the mysterious man was can only be speculation, however. The fact remains that too little concrete data is known of the man to allow a complete and specific picture of his life. But Robert Christian did leave behind an invaluable tool to aid the ongoing pursuit of an understanding of his character and motivations. The bulk of the book that he wrote and published in 1986 is devoted to the relation of Christian's political, social, and philosophical ideas. Many of his proposals are now outdated or made irrelevant by the introduction of new information or infrastructure into human society in the time between the book's publication and today. But though its utility as a potential resource for policymakers may have diminished, it remains quite pertinent to the discussion of the Georgia Guidestones and their author.

THOUGHTS ON RELIGION

The chapters of *Common Sense Renewed* divide Christian's ideas into several different rough categories: religion, domestic social problems, and foreign affairs—with specific regard to Cold War era politics and concerns. Each of these sections reveals a little more about the character of the man who wrote them, and when viewed together a more complete picture begins to emerge.

The tenth chapter of the book, entitled "Reflections on God and Religion," summarizes his somewhat complex theological ideas. It is worth noting that when Christian described himself to Joe Fendley and Wyatt Martin, he said that he was "a follower of the teachings of Jesus Christ,"[155] but, despite his pseudonym, he never actually referred to himself as a "Christian." This may seem at first to be a semantic point, but viewed in the light of the more specific iterations of his belief structure that are outlined in "Reflections on God and Religion," it appears to be an essential distinction.

Many of Robert Christian's religious ideas fit well within the bounds of the modern sects of Christianity. He professes to believe in a single, benevolent God. He believes that two thousand years ago a man named Jesus performed miracles and influenced others with his faith and his philosophy, and that same man was put to death for his works. Yet Christian does not choose to self-identify as a member of any particular church. It is possible that this decision to eschew sectarian classifications was as a direct result of his stance on religious tolerance, as in his book he states that "it is apparent that no religion has a monopoly on truth,"[156] and he encourages people of differing religious viewpoints to attempt to understand and accept one another.

In refusing to label himself with a specific spiritual viewpoint, he may have been attempting to emphasize his tolerant ideals, but it is also possible that he genuinely did not feel a kinship with any of the organized forms of Christianity. Some of R. C. Christian's ideas seem to be at odds with the conventional standards held by most Christians. The various sects of Christianity interpret the Bible in different ways, but without exception they hold it to be the true and accurate Word of God. Christian, however, holds a more flexible view.

> Appropriate humility suggests that we regard all our knowledge as incomplete and tentative, ever subject to revision in the light of new information.[157]

> … our understanding of God is distorted and inadequate. We continue to use ancient concepts because of habit and because we lack good substitutes. Many wise people concede that God is almost completely unknowable for human minds and senses.[158]

In these passages Christian maintains that religious knowledge is subjective and malleable, implying that it is quite possible that many people, including himself, may prove to be incorrect in their assessments of the divine. This assertion, while couched in inoffensive terms, nevertheless stands in direct opposition to the viewpoints of the leaders of the various Judeo-Christian faiths and of other entities who consider themselves to be in possession of absolute truths.

Christian also indicates a dislike for religious dogma or ritual that he considers to be no longer relevant or appropriate in a modern setting. He highlights the fact that most of the major religions codified their ideas and rites at a time long past for a people and a culture long dead. The failure to update traditions to match the constantly evolving body of human knowledge has, he asserts, subjected religion in general to "criticism, and sometimes to ridicule."[159] In a sense, with this statement he speaks out against organized religion in general, as conservative traditionalism has been a fundamental quality of nearly all of the major world religions.

The overarching theme that pervades the entirety of *Common Sense Renewed* is the supremacy of human reason, and the chapter that discusses religion is no exception to this. In stark contrast to the standard doctrines of Christianity, which hold that faith is the final authority, Christian firmly asserts that emotional and intuitive reactions should only be considered after they have been examined by the intellect:

There is a legitimate place for inspired teach-

> ings by religious leaders who may through intuition or inspiration perceive concepts which lie beyond the reach of human reason and scientific proof. So long as those teachings do not conflict with our reasoned judgments and so long as they contribute to human happiness they can be accepted on faith.[160]
>
> So long as we do not permit faith to *override* our rational powers we should use those talents to explore the frontiers which lie at the outer limits of scientific observation.[161]

This idea of using reason, not faith, as the touchstone for all other beliefs is much more reminiscent of the tenets of Deism than of any of the varieties of modern Christianity.

Though Deism has roots that go back as far as the ancient Greek philosophers, it was at the height of its popularity during the Enlightenment of the seventeenth and eighteenth centuries in Europe. Deists hold that the existence of a supreme being can be determined in a rational way by the application of reason, and that even that deity is subject to the natural laws of the universe. Christian echoes this idea at several points in his book:

> Perhaps we are like cells in the mind of God, contributing to celestial functions beyond our ken, just as our cells unknowingly fashion our thoughts and actions. Perhaps the laws of na-

> ture order and constrain even the living and eternal Deity from which they spring, and of which they are a part.[162]

Judeo-Christian dogma commands belief in an omnipotent God who is not limited by laws of any kind. Christian's writings, by contrast, are more consistent with Deistic beliefs on this matter.

R. C. Christian also connects himself with Deism by his many allusions to Thomas Paine and his works. As noted previously, the title of Christian's book, *Common Sense Renewed*, is a clear reference to Paine's seminal work, *Common Sense*. Christian also pulls a quotation from Paine's *The Rights of Man* in his own chapter about human reproduction. And throughout *Common Sense Renewed*, Christian reiterates time and again that what he seeks to bring about is an "Age of Reason."

In 1794, Thomas Paine published the first part of a three-part pamphlet entitled *The Age of Reason*. In this work, Paine outlined many of the common Deist arguments of the day in a bold and accessible style. Its effects on society at the time were huge and far-reaching. In subsequent years, other thinkers and authors latched on to the phrase, "the age of reason," and began to use it to describe alternately the period of the Western Enlightenment and a theoretical future point in time in which human reason was the authority on which all decisions and plans were made. It is in this latter sense that Christian makes frequent use of the phrase.

Along the four sides of the capstone of the Georgia Guidestones, in four ancient languages, the words "Let these be guidestones to an Age of Reason" are engraved. In Christian's book, he states that the Guidestones were meant to "hasten in small ways the dawning of an age of reason."[163] Chapters one, three, four, nine, and twelve of *Common Sense Renewed* all end with the words "Age of Reason," and chapter eight is entitled "A Beginning for the Age of Reason." Every single chapter employs the phrase at least once. And there are a variety of similarities in the content of *Common Sense Renewed* and *The Age of Reason* as well.

The motivations behind both treatises were born of parallel circumstances. At the beginning of "Reflections on God and Religion," R. C. Christian mentions that in most of the communist nations of his time, atheism had become the state-mandated "religion." The following chapter, "On the Conversion of Russia," speaks at length about the ways in which the communist atheists could be persuaded to hold on to certain vestiges of spirituality. In order to do this, he asserts that it would be necessary to reevaluate the major religions of the world in a rational, reasoned light and to extract from them the basic core principles that they have in common. Those principles would then be presented as a universal code of human ethics.

At the beginning of *The Age of Reason*, Paine outlines his reason for the publication of his pamphlets.

> The circumstance that has now taken place in France of the total abolition of the whole national order of priesthood, and of everything

> appertaining to compulsive systems of religion, and compulsive articles of faith, has not only precipitated my intention, but rendered a work of this kind exceedingly necessary, lest in the general wreck of superstition, of false systems of government, and false theology, we lose sight of morality, of humanity, and of the theology that is true.[164]

Disturbed by the effects that the French Revolution was having on the population's general spirituality, Paine also felt the need to express his opinions on religion. He intended to show to the French that religious belief could be comprised of more than just the tradition and corruption that they perceived in the Catholic Church of the time, and that even religion could be dealt with rationally.

But it is not only Paine's motivations that Christian echoes, but also some of his ideas. Christian saw problems with the established scriptures with respect to attempting to convert others because in their attempts to express truths clearly, they frequently used contradictory language.

> Ancient writings which still play a prominent role in religions of the Judeo-Christian-Muslim tradition sometimes describe God as stern, righteous by human standards, vindictive, unforgiving and tyrannical. At other times God is represented as all-wise, loving, solicitous

> for our welfare, and forgiving of our failings. These conflicting interpretations reveal the inadequacy and confusion of our attempts to describe the true nature of the Supreme Being.[165]

Paine observed the same issues of inconsistency, though his language is much more hostile towards Christianity, and the conclusions that he reaches seem to differ somewhat from Christian's:

> Putting aside everything that might excite laughter by its absurdity, or detestation by its profaneness, and confining ourselves merely to an examination of the parts, it is impossible to conceive a story more derogatory to the Almighty, more inconsistent with his wisdom, more contradictory to his power, than [the Bible] is.[166]

At the time that Paine was writing, corruption and intolerance were still rampant problems within the body of the Church. His vehement, almost disgusted language with respect to Christianity is partially a reaction to these problems and partially a rhetorical device that he used in order to appeal to the common man. Christian obviously had fewer harsh feelings towards Christianity, and indeed embraced some elements of it, and thus chose a more affable tone for his criticisms.

Despite Paine's seeming disrespect for Judeo-Christian thought, he, like most Deists of the time, shared Christian's feelings on religious tolerance. In the dedicatory introduction of *The Age of Reason*, which he addressed to the citizens of the United States, Paine stated:

> I put the following work under your protection. It contains my opinions upon Religion. You will do me the justice to remember, that I have always strenuously supported the Right of every Man to his own opinion, however different that opinion might be to mine. He who denies to another this right, makes a slave of himself to his present opinion, because he precludes himself the right of changing it.[167]

Open-minded ideas of this kind, while fairly commonplace in the modern West, were quite new and rare in Paine's day. Irreverent and ostentatious though he may have been, Paine was undeniably an important figure of the Enlightenment, and he seems to have had a strong effect on Christian's thoughts and work.

IDEAS FOR THE IMPROVEMENT OF SOCIETY

"Human intelligence," Robert Christian felt, "is capable of devising solutions to all our problems—war, population control, justice under law, and the progressive improvement and perfection of our species as the shepherd of life on earth."[168] His intelligence led him to formulate courses of action that he felt could resolve all of those issues. He believed so fully in the potential power of his proposals that he committed them to paper in *Common Sense Renewed* and sent copies of his book to thousands of political leaders the world over at his own expense.

Ideas that a person holds so dearly that he is willing to act on them, even when doing so is inconvenient and comes at great personal cost, are almost certain to be integral to that person's sense of self. So while a person's political stance does not always necessarily reveal much about his character, in Christian's case his beliefs on social and cultural change can be used to dissipate some of the fog of mystery that surrounds his identity.

Based upon the platform that he outlines in his book, we can infer that, if R. C. Christian were still alive today, he would most likely vote like a Republican with strong libertarian leanings. Most of the plans that he lays out to combat America's ills are very much in keeping with a strictly conservative domestic policy. In general, he adopts the stance that the major ills facing the United States have their roots in "too much government"[169] and the naiveté of politicians who fail to see that the persistence of a large national debt will eventually put the country at a severe global disadvantage.

Many of his ideas and complaints are familiar to any modern American who has recently tuned in to Fox News. He scorns the lack of stricture with which the U.S. polices its borders. He calls for stronger sanctions on employers who knowingly provide jobs to illegal immigrants, and suggests that "idle but able-bodied Americans"[170] ought to perform those jobs, even if they consider them to be "below their social station, or … esthetically distasteful."[171] He condemns the removal of all traces of religion and spirituality from public schools and enjoins districts to introduce a generalized code of moral conduct into the perceived ethical vacuum in the educational system.

Christian calls for the abolition of the minimum wage and of labor regulations that "hamper our productive efforts."[172] He laments the many other laws that dictate the internal policies of corporate entities, saying that though they are well-meaning, they "are a direct cause for increased costs,"[173] which in turn impedes America's ability to remain globally competitive. He speaks longingly of a time when "'profit' was not a nasty word."[174] A substantial portion of the text dealing with socio-economic issues is focused on commercial regulations.

Mixed in with his run-of-the-mill socially conservative ideas, however, are some suggestions that are a good bit more unusual. He proposes that universities and technical colleges restrict the enrollment of students in various areas of concentration based upon projections of actual need for careers in their related fields. He advises the creation of a nationally-funded railway network in order to provide incentives for distributors to do more of their shipping across rails instead of the highways, thereby relieving congestion and stress on roads and easing some of the energy burden away from petroleum and onto coal. He recommends the creation and implementation of a new, worldwide language to aid both trade and peaceful relations.

Most noteworthy, however, are Christian's proposals challenging some of our society's standard ideas of personal freedom. His suggestion that unemployment benefits be eliminated is, by itself, not far out of the ordinary. But Christian goes one step further, stating that unemployed individuals should be forced to relocate to areas of higher employment availability within the country, regardless of the distance involved. "An illiterate Mexican or Jamaican citizen will travel thousands of miles eagerly to seek ... employment," he asserts; "unemployed Americans should be *required* to make similar efforts."[175] Such a scenario would certainly ruffle many feathers if implemented, but Christian counters that "Americans have grown accustomed to the comfortable living standards based upon our once abundant resources. We are inclined to take them for granted."[176] This then, he hoped, would perhaps engender more of an appreciation for that standard of living.

Even more unconventional is his position on healthcare. In a very brief section of the text, Christian discusses the problems of the rising costs of medical procedures and concludes that it will be necessary to limit the amount of care that is distributed.

> We simply cannot afford to replace every failing heart with a pump or transplant ... It will be necessary for well informed citizens to work with knowledgeable physicians in establishing guidelines that will make possible a reasonable allocation or "rationing" of the care that we can collectively afford, favoring those individuals whose continuing lives are most valuable to society at large.[177]

It is the last part of his assessment that would likely be most controversial. In recent years, discussions about how health-care should be monitored or managed in America have shown that many people have very strong feelings on the subject. Undoubtedly, this was true during Christian's time as well, but the anonymous man did not compromise his approach of using reason to determine policy merely to avoid controversy at any point in his book, and this was no exception.

Many of Christian's ideas for the improvement of the social and economic structures of the United States are unconventional, but they are nevertheless quite interesting. The most original of these proposals seem to indicate, if nothing else, that he was a man who spent a lot of time thinking about the problems that plagued his society, and that he could not have contented himself until he made an attempt to foster constructive changes in the system that produced those problems. The Guidestones were a part of that attempt, and *Common Sense Renewed* was another. Any further steps he may have taken were not associated with the same pseudonym, so it is impossible to know what they may have been.

Very little is presently known about the identity of the man who erected the Guidestones. Indeed it is quite possible that further biographical information will never surface to shed light on his motivations. But his identity is only part of the story. The context and circumstances of the time in which he lived also heavily influenced Christian's decision to create the Guidestones. About that time period there is substantially more information.

13. Structural damage to English face (top right corner)—
evidence of an apparent attempt to topple the monument

CHAPTER 6:

ALTERNATIVES TO ARMAGEDDON

It is the summer of 1979.

It has been thirty-four years since the world first bore witness to the devastating effects of nuclear weaponry. Between 150,000 and 246,000 people perished in the bombings of Hiroshima and Nagasaki.[178] Though the exact details of the events were hidden from the public eye for many years, it is now widely known that the atomic bombs visited horrors upon the people of those cities, the like of which had never been seen before. It is also widely known that the global stockpile of nuclear weapons is both much more numerous and much more powerful now than it was in 1945.

It has been twenty-three years since the Soviet premier, Nikita Khrushchev, told the ambassadors of Western capitalist countries, "We will bury you!"[179] in a shocking alleged slip of the tongue that nevertheless chilled all who heard it. The USSR has made it abundantly clear that they have little to no use for non-communist nations, and that they have the military might to, at least on occasion, silence them.

It has been seventeen years since the brinksmanship of the Cuban Missile Crisis nearly triggered a thermonuclear war, and that danger is still a possibility. After a few hopeful years of détente, relations between the United States and the Soviet Union are becoming strained once again as Soviet-backed communist uprisings in other countries threaten to tip the shaky balance of control between the rival superpowers.

It has been just over a year since the Afghan people executed Mohammad Daoud Khan, who had been their president, and replaced him with a member of their communist party. In six months the Soviet Army will invade Afghanistan to solidify the newly reformed government, triggering intense fear and unease in the West in the process.

It is the summer of 1979, and for three decades the West has lived with the uneasy knowledge that the Soviet Union has "The Bomb."

THE COLD WAR MIND-SET

In America today it is nearly impossible for even those who were adults during the Cold War to fully remember the specter of dread that pervaded the era. Today, fallout shelters are kitschy curiosities, and instructional films like *Duck and Cover* are subjects of fun. Movies and books that depict wars with Russia are viewed with nostalgia or sometimes even amusement. The threat appears to have passed. The Berlin Wall has fallen, the Soviet Union has disbanded, and the United States Department of Defense has turned its eyes to other matters.

Since the events of September 11, 2001, the watchword has been "terrorism," and many Americans are preoccupied with fears that other small groups of fanatics will detonate explosives in other crowded areas. These fears are real, and their effects are felt in modern society, but they are of a different species than the fears felt by society between 1949 and 1989. Because the worry in those days was not that a few thousand people would be murdered by a madman, but that perhaps the entire population of the world would be decimated in a crossfire of nuclear missiles. For many people, this was not merely a possibility, but an inevitability.

For R. C. Christian as for other politically conscious people of the time, the prospect of a full-scale nuclear war seemed more and more likely. The arms race engendered by the doctrine of Mutually Assured Destruction had resulted in an unprecedented build-up of weapons in both the USSR and the United States. In 1949, there were only 246 nuclear warheads worldwide, but by 1979, there were 24,107 missiles in the U.S. stockpile and nearly 28,000 in the USSR. France, China and the United Kingdom each possessed modest nuclear arsenals by that point as well, bringing the global total to well over 50,000 atomic warheads.[180] Many of these bombs were actively deployed at all times, shuttling back and forth from their fail-safe points, waiting for the moment they were ordered to drop their payloads.

The idea that the Cold War could somehow reach a peaceful resolution without any bloodshed seemed increasingly naïve. Neither side was showing any signs of backing away from the hostilities. The conflict escalated tirelessly, and it seemed as though nuclear war would one day be unavoidable.

Robert Christian was a worldly man who was not only aware of current events, but also felt the need to act upon them. When faced with danger, it is only natural for a person to take measures to protect himself, but Christian evidently felt that he had a stake in not only his own well-being but that of mankind in general. So while he probably built a fallout shelter for himself and his family in his backyard, he also took steps to attempt to build a fallout shelter for civilization itself.

He built a monument that he intended would "convey certain ideas across time to others."[181] In the years since the monument was built, many people have disagreed with those ideas, but Christian believed that their implementation could lead to a better, more peaceful and balanced civilization in the future. To clarify and disseminate his ideas, he wrote a book and distributed it to thousands of political leaders the world over in the hopes that they could take the steps required to avert a nuclear holocaust. But should the worst occur, the Georgia Guidestones, strategically located "away from the main tourist centers" and in a "generally mild climate,"[182] would likely endure the catastrophe and live on to advise future generations on how to avoid the mistakes of their predecessors.

THOUGHTS ON FOREIGN POLICY

Christian believed war had become a barbaric anachronism that had no place in modern society. He lamented that man's great capacity for reason had not been exercised in this area:

> We live in a time of great peril. Humanity and the proud achievements of its infancy on earth

> are in grave danger. Our knowledge has outstripped wisdom ... We have advanced our knowledge of the natural sciences but have not adequately controlled our baser animal instincts. We have begun to accept the rule of law but have limited its application, permitting it to regulate the affairs of individuals and of small political divisions while we neglect to use it in controlling major aggression. We have outlawed the use of murder and violence in resolving individual disputes, but have failed to develop procedures to peacefully settle conflicts between nations.[183]

Many of his ideas for developing a better global society centered around this core theme of eschewing violence in favor of reasoned discussion.

The sixth tenet etched into the Guidestones, "Let all nations rule internally, resolving external disputes in a world court," addresses this explicitly. It was Christian's belief that the development of an international institution specifically designed to enable nations to resolve their disputes and handle their grievances with one another through mediated discussion could eliminate the need for war. Certain simple, generalized global laws would dictate the conduct of the countries of the Earth, and this court would enforce them. The result, he hoped, would be something similar to the original intentions behind the United Nations, but that would be unhampered by the diplomatic restrictions and unchecked veto powers that obstruct the UN's effectiveness.

The main barriers, as Christian saw it, to the creation of such an institution were the seemingly irreconcilable differences between capitalist and communist social and judicial systems. Russian communism, he felt, allowed too much power to be in the hands of too few people and was not responsive enough to the needs of the populace at large. He also asserted, however, that some of the criticisms of American capitalism were valid, and that certain checks needed to be applied to the system to prevent abuses. While he did not expect either the Soviet Union or the United States to make any fundamental changes to their respective political systems, he felt that they might be motivated to come to some compromises, as "thinking people in both nations must soon realize the futility of continuing the 'cold war' and its attendant arms race."[184]

Christian primarily outlines his ideas for these compromises in two of the chapters in *Common Sense Renewed*, "A Beginning for the Age of Reason" and "To Make Partners of Rivals." As an opening conciliatory gesture, he recommends that the future home of the "World Congress of Reason" be situated in Russia, so as to balance the fact that the United Nations is headquartered in New York. But he goes on to indicate that the Soviets must separate themselves from the core objective of converting all of the countries of the world to communist political systems, by force if necessary. This goal, he says, prohibits the United States from being able to trust the Soviets not to attempt to sow dissent within its own boundaries, and thereby prohibits peace.

He also recommends that the Soviets inject a small element of democracy into their present system, allowing members of certain collectives or workers at factories to elect representatives who would then become party members. He then suggests that the party members would vote to select the nominees that were then put forward on the unopposed ballots to the people. This, he asserts, would allow the public some measure of voice in the policies that shape their lives without disrupting the general tone and structure of the political system in the USSR. Controversially, Christian even suggests that this or another system of limited suffrage might prove to be better than the American democratic system, which he feels is sometimes disrupted by unintelligent or uninformed voters:

> A "selective democracy" sustained through suffrage standards of a high order, using the mechanism of the Communist Party may ultimately prove to be a superior form of government. If political power is transmitted from the people to those in ruling positions in a manner which reflects knowledge and understanding by those who participate in elections, government of the people by the best representatives of the people may become a reality.[185]

The same criticisms of American democracy are expanded upon in his chapter "Suffrage in the United States," where Christian asserts that a person should be required to provide both "proof of understanding of our government and its history" and "evidence of economic productivity"[186] in order to earn his vote.

Christian perceived other flaws in the American system as well, however. He alleged that one byproduct of capitalism, inherited wealth, was an exceedingly great threat to effectual democracy, comparing the situation it creates to that of an aristocracy. "There is merit," he asserts, "in permitting enterprising individuals to enjoy the fruits of their labor throughout their lives. It is more difficult to justify the transferral of that wealth to others who have not contributed in any way to its creation."[187] To resolve this problem, Christian suggests that, upon their deaths, exceedingly wealthy people only be allowed to leave behind modest sums to support any surviving spouses or children, and that the rest of their wealth be confiscated or reinvested by the state. He felt that this would remove the threat of an entrenched, powerful upper-class and increase economic mobility in America.

Other, more minor proposals are put forward to the Soviets and Americans for ways to make their respective systems of government more harmonious with one another, but Christian stresses that there is really only one thing that the two nations need agree on in order to make his system work:

> Leaders in both countries should jointly develop an international philosophy whereby a variety of political and economic systems can coexist in friendly competition ... Political patterns will undergo endless change in

> the future. We should not attempt to fit all nations to one pattern. No system is suited to all future time. If America and the Soviet Union will agree on this basic premise, together they can lead the world in a new, nonviolent, revolution that will make reason and compassion the guiding forces of humanity.[188]

A FALLOUT SHELTER FOR CIVILIZATION

Many of the ideas that Robert Christian puts forth with respect to Soviet-American relations are no longer relevant in the post-Cold-War world. The Soviet Union has collapsed, and communism of the type that was practiced within its borders is seldom found in the world today. But these chapters of his book are far from useless for one who is searching for Christian's purpose in creating the Georgia Guidestones—they are essential.

From these pages it is abundantly clear that this anonymous man's mind was much preoccupied with world affairs during this period. He composed an entire book detailing his thoughts on how to resolve the crisis of the Cold War, and his chapter on the creation of the Guidestones is seamlessly a part of it. Christian's opinion of the military struggles of nations is inexorably tied to his motivation in commissioning the monument. "His thoughts," Wyatt Martin claims, "were that [the Guidestones] would more or less help people to reestablish

... civilization if we became stupid enough to annihilate each other with atomic weapons."[189]

The people who have visited the Guidestones in their humble setting in the time since the Cold War ended have often walked away from the landmark confused. Without the historical context in which they were conceived, the stones tell an incomplete story, and it is difficult for a person in current times to understand what could possibly motivate a man to anonymously erect a monument engraved with guidelines for the conduct of nations. Many of them have supposed sinister ulterior motives in the absence of any apparent evidence of intent.

But from the writings he left behind, it seems clear that the mysterious R. C. Christian was just a man frightened for his world. He watched events unfold around him that were dangerous to all of mankind, events that he was powerless to control, and he felt the need to do something to advance the ideas that he felt might make things right. Those ideas are themselves in many cases controversial, but whatever their actual merits, Christian at least seemed to genuinely believe that they would improve the state of mankind.

Whatever his name, he was a man, and his intentions were good. He acted upon his conscience and undertook a project that was massive in both scale and cost, all in the name of trying to create a better world. His opinions on that better world still stand on a hill looking down on Elberton, Georgia, with the contrary opinions of others scrawled across them in paint and epoxy. The merits of those differing opinions are not quantifiable, but the mediums of their expression seem to differ vastly in quality.

But perhaps the next visitor to the Guidestones who disagrees with the message he sees will be inspired, not to inhibit the expression of Christian's ideas about how to better mankind, but to express his own publicly as well. And perhaps through the open and constructive discourse of such lofty thoughts we can indeed find the pathway to a better world.

14. Workers at the Pyramid Quarry extracting granite blocks for the Guidestones project

AFTERWORD

In 1898, the tiny town of Elberton, Georgia opened its first granite finishing plant. Though there had been a commercial quarry in the area for nine years, prior to this point the city had never produced any monuments from its granite. But the women of the Confederate Memorial Association were determined to change that.

Early in the year the CMA approached an Italian sculptor by the name of Arthur Beter and commissioned a statue to commemorate the Confederate soldiers who had died in the Civil War. The Elberton Granite and Marble Works plant was opened shortly thereafter in order to polish and shape the statue and its fifteen-foot-tall pedestal. And on July 15, 1898, the memorial was at last revealed to an eager crowd of onlookers amidst much pomp and circumstance.

But the monument that the people of Elberton set their eyes upon that Friday morning was not at all what they had expected.

All in attendance agreed that the pedestal of the structure was very finely crafted. An engraving of a Confederate battle flag with one tattered edge sat upon the column, and beneath it were carved the words, "Elbert County to her Confederate Dead." Crossed swords and small stacks of ammunition adorned other faces of the base. Further inscriptions gave voice to the proud feelings the community shared for the soldiers they had lost in the war.

The statue that stood atop this fine platform, however,

was quite another matter. Though he was seven feet tall, the granite soldier somehow managed to look "short and squatty."[190] His legs and feet were abnormally wide, causing one writer for *The Elberton Star* to observe that he must have been afflicted with gout. His face was strangely rounded, his eyes just a bit too wide, and his mustache was broad and upturned like that of a British imperial officer in Victorian Africa.

But to the minds of the townspeople, the greatest affront was in the soldier's apparel. Instead of the mid-thigh-length light jacket and flop hat that were more common to the uniform of the Confederate soldier, the statue was depicted in a knee-length coat, cape, and bill cap. While the exact style and specifications of the uniforms of both sides in the Civil War tended to vary quite widely due to limited resources, the living Confederate veterans of Elberton all seemed to agree that this statue looked for all the world like a Union soldier.

It was generally believed by the townsfolk that such a massive discrepancy could be no error, and so the sculptor, Arthur Beter, was taunted and called a Yankee sympathizer. But those citizens' modern counterparts now admit that as Beter was a very recent immigrant to the country, it was also quite possible that he simply did not know what a Confederate soldier looked like.

One observer quipped that the statue looked like a "cross between a Pennsylvania Dutchman and a hippopotamus,"[191] and so the people of Elbert County began referring to him as "Old Dutchy," and he was not much loved. The general ire and indignation of the townspeople grew until finally, two years later, it reached fever pitch.

On the morning of August 14, 1900, the city of Elberton woke to find that one of their number had removed Dutchy from his honored place. The granite figure lay in several pieces at the foot of its pedestal, with its legs broken off and a noose about its neck. No one mourned his loss.

Two days later, *The Elberton Star* reported the incident glibly: "Dutchy is no more. The man with the stony glare in his eyes took a tumble Monday night and is now lying in the middle of the square with two broken limbs."[192] The article went on to give a facetious account of the circumstances leading up to Dutchy's demise, indicating that the statue had fainted and fallen backwards due to heat-exhaustion induced by his overwarm clothing and his strong desire for a keg of beer. Concluding with a more serious tone, the author noted the following:

> It is not known who pulled the figure down, but it is generally conceded that their conduct was not meant as an insult to the Confederate veterans or to the ladies or to anyone connected to the monument. It was simply an eyesore and they wanted to get rid of it and have a more appropriate Confederate monument in its place.[193]

Dutchy lay where he had fallen until August 16, when a crowd of people gathered once again and buried the granite man in front of his pedestal in the center of town square. After a few years, another sculptor produced a second statue to complete the memorial, and the city of Elberton all but forgot about Old Dutchy.

When people examine a work of art, whether it be a monument, a novel, or an oil painting, they naturally attempt to discern its meaning. But this is not always the easiest of prospects, as what makes an artwork distinctive from other instances of expression and communication is that art expresses its ideas relatively abstractly. Rather than state in plain language what it is that he is trying to say, an artist plays with stone, paint, light, or other mediums in order to hint at or allude to his meaning. There are a variety of subjects that are historically difficult to convey ideas about in a straightforward way; emotional and spiritual concepts are, by their very natures, outside the bounds of strictly logical and analytical thinking. For these themes in particular, it can be beneficial to take an artistic approach to self-expression to attempt to transmit one's thoughts and experiences to others. But the very same vagueness that allows an artist to discuss ideas that he might otherwise be unable to articulate also allows for a variety of interpretation by his audience that is sometimes very wide indeed.

In literary and visual art criticism, scholars have widely debated whether or not the meaning that the artist intended is the most important aspect of the work. Within the modern school of New Criticism, this idea is referred to as the "intentional fallacy" and is derided as not only incorrect but also impossible. Critics such as W. K. Wimsatt and Monroe Beardsley have asserted that "the design or intention of the author is neither available nor desirable as a standard"[194] for evaluating a work. They claim that it is impossible to ever fully ascertain the exact authorial intent, and that even if it was obtainable it is not worth considering, as to do so would only distract one from the work itself.

Scholars in other schools of thought, such as Psychoanalytic, Marxist, or Feminist Criticism, dispute the idea that the author's ideas about his work are irrelevant, but even they do not disagree that it can be difficult to ascertain what exactly those ideas are. And no art critic has ever asserted that the authorial intent is the only standard upon which the art should be judged. The content of the piece must always be considered on its own merits as well.

In the case of the Georgia Guidestones, the mystery that surrounds the artist's identity has caused many to fixate upon the authorial intent of the piece exclusively. Conspiracy theorists such as Mark Dice and Van Smith have focused most of their efforts and study of the monument around attempting to discern who R. C. Christian was and what his motivations were for commissioning such a strange structure. But Christian's perspective on what the Guidestones mean is only one among a great many opinions.

For Old Dutchy, the situation was reversed. The people of Elbert County had little care for what Arthur Beter intended to convey when he carved his "squatty" soldier. They looked at it, and they saw an ugly figure who reminded them of their enemies. And they tore it down.

But Dutchy's story did not end there.

In 1982, the Elberton Granite Association decided to go looking for the town's most historically despised monument. He had been the stuff of legend around Elberton ever since his demise and hasty burial over eighty years before. His replacement had languished for several decades atop his old pedestal, and there were many in the town who did not believe that the short little fellow had ever existed. So on April 19, a team of contracted construction workers took to the square to see what they could find.

Coincidentally, the effort was led by the same man who had sold a tract of his land to a mysterious stranger looking for a home for the Georgia Guidestones, Mr. Wayne Mullenix. Mullenix and his men dug into the earth in front of the memorial for two hours without result. "Hopes began to fade," recalls Hudson Cone, who was present on that "red-letter day." But at last, they found what they sought.

Entombed in the hard Georgia red clay were indeed the pieces of a seven-foot statue of a soldier. A throng of curious townsfolk looked on in interest as the team completed the excavation process. Dutchy was filthy, encrusted with the brilliant red-orange soil that had been his home for the better part of a century, and so they loaded him onto the bed of a large truck with a crane and drove him through the local car wash to clean up.

But after he was rinsed off, the representatives from the EGA discovered something amazing. Underneath all of the dirt, the sculpture was in near perfect condition. Despite being thrown to the ground and then buried for eighty-two years, the surface of the granite remained unblemished and un-weathered.

The reception that Dutchy received now was a far cry from the outrage that the town had felt for him before. No longer was he seen as a gouty Yankee, but as "a remarkable advertisement for our Elberton Granite."[195] The EGA considered trying to replace Dutchy on a pedestal in the square, but they could think of no safe way to do this. He was "so heavy," Cone says, that they could not be certain he would not just fall down again. So instead, they devoted an entire room to him in the Elberton Granite Museum and set him out in the center of it, surrounding the redeemed Dutchy with articles and videos about his history.

Perspectives on artistic works are both subjective and malleable. The significance that one generation or social group derives from a given piece can be completely different from the meanings that other groups might find. The people of Elbert County in the early nineteenth century saw Old Dutchy as an offensive eyesore, where the citizens now see it as a proud part of their heritage. By and large, those same people see the Georgia Guidestones in a similar way.

Visitors to the Guidestones have come away with a variety of impressions of the monument. Some see the ideas it presents as a threatening and sinister manifesto, while others take a more positive approach to the landmark, feeling that it spreads a message of peace in a world troubled by war.

Christian himself seemed to be of the latter opinion.

But not one of these perspectives is more valid than another. The Guidestones, like any work of art, presents a "prism of meaning"[196] to those who would regard it. Its value is in the fact that it is open to personal interpretation, and that it engenders discussion about the ways in which those interpretations differ.

Now, decades after the end of the Cold War, devastating nuclear war is still a very real possibility, but it has lost much of its impact on the popular consciousness. Works of art about the subject, like the Georgia Guidestones, help to maintain a dialogue about the state of global affairs and the prospect of a more peaceful world. Those who read the precepts put forth on the monument are affected in some way by what they say. They debate the merits of the proposals, in their own minds or aloud, and they come away from the experience thinking about issues that they might otherwise not have considered. And even if one does not believe that this is what R. C. Christian intended when he designed the work, the effect remains.

But there are many who have called for the monument's destruction, and there are some who have themselves tried to exact that destruction. Seeing it as a symbol for things that they violently oppose, they have obscured its message and attempted to break its stones.

No good can come of such actions. Were the Guidestones to be torn down, after a time they would likely go unremembered, and the dialogue about the merits of the embedded ideas would end. For both those who oppose the message they see in its granite faces and those who support it, this would not be a positive thing. The opportunity for discussion and the exchange of ideas would be lost, and so too would be the possibility of a resolution that pleased all parties.

Instead, perhaps those wishing to endorse a counterpoint could create similar works of art, in Elberton or elsewhere, expressing their own ideas on how to usher in a better tomorrow. Perhaps if there were more such things the dialogue would grow even larger and real change could occur.

For now, the Georgia Guidestones remain, and R. C. Christian's message continues to speak to those who listen. Christian himself hoped that this message could help ease human suffering. He hoped to create a better world.

> The guides are not religious. They are not commandments. We have no authority to command. Affirmation of our thoughts can only occur as they are endorsed and supported by the reasoned judgment of this and future generations. We invite human beings of all persuasions to consider them with open minds, adapting them to the changing circumstances of unknown future centuries.
>
> —Robert Christian, 1986

ENDNOTES

CHAPTER 1: THE GEORGIA GUIDESTONES

1 Elberton Granite Finishing Co., Inc. "The Georgia Guidestones," *The Sun*, Hartwell, GA, 1981.

2 *Ibid.*, p. 5.

3 *Ibid.*

4 Sullivan, Randall. *Wired Magazine*, "American Stonehenge: Monumental Instructions for the Post-Apocalypse," April 20, 2009, p. 2.

5 Elberton Granite Finishing Co., Inc. "The Georgia Guidestones," p. 11.

6 Sullivan. "American Stonehenge," p. 3.

7 *Ibid.*

8 Christian, Robert. *Common Sense Renewed.* Stoyles Graphic Services, Lake Mills, Iowa, 1986, p. 8.

9 Elberton Granite Finishing Co., Inc. "The Georgia Guidestones," p. 10.

10 Christian. *Common Sense Renewed.* p. 8.

11 Elberton Granite Finishing Co., Inc. "The Georgia Guidestones," p. 5.

12 Wyatt Martin. *The Guidestones*, Dir. Noel Brown, 2011.

13 Christian. *Common Sense Renewed*, "About This Book."

14 Elberton Granite Finishing Co., Inc. "The Georgia Guidestones," p. 19.

15 *Ibid.*, p. 39.

CHAPTER 2: THE GRANITE CAPITAL OF THE WORLD

16 United States Census. 2008, Population Estimates.

17 Lewis, Boyd. "Mystery in Stone: A monument, a vision, or home base for Witches?" *Brown's Guide to Georgia*, August 1980, p. 60.

18 *Ibid.*, p. 62.

19 *Ibid.*

20 Martin. *The Guidestones.*

21 *Ibid.*

22 Lewis. "Mystery in Stone," p. 62.

23 Lipsey, Paul. "Guidestones: Are These Stones a Monument to Mankind Or, as Some Fear, A Temple for Cult Worship?" *The Elberton Star*, August 1, 1980.

24 *Ibid.*

25 *Ibid.*

26 *Ibid.*

27 Tom Robinson. "Episode 8 – Ten Commandments of the New World Order," *Out There Radio*. http://outthereradio.net/posts/episode-8-the-georgia-guidestones.

28 Lewis. "Mystery in Stone," p. 61.

29 *Ibid.*

30 *Ibid.*

31 *Ibid.*

32 *Ibid.*

33 Martin. *The Guidestones.*

34 Lewis. "Mystery in Stone," pp. 61–62.

35 Osinski, Bill. "Mr. Christian, come here!" *The Atlanta Journal Constitution*, August 31, 1997.

36 Lewis. "Mystery in Stone," p. 60.

37 *Ibid.*, p. 59.

38 *Ibid.*, p. 60.

39 *Ibid.*

40 Robinson. *Out There Radio.*

41 Osinski. "Mr. Christian, come here!"

CHAPTER 3: ROSES, ROSES, ROSES

42 Lewis. "Mystery in Stone," p. 62.

43 Jodi Minogue. "Episode 8 – Ten Commandments of the New World Order," *Out There Radio.*

44 Lewis. "Mystery in Stone," p. 62.

45 *Ibid.*

46 *Ibid.*

47 *Ibid.*

48 *Ibid.*

49 Randall Carlson. Unpublished interview.

50 *Ibid.*

51 Agrippa, Henry Cornelius. *Three Books of Occult Philosophy*, p. 711. trans. James Freake. Llewellyn Publications. St. Paul, MN, 1998.

52 Lewis. "Mystery in Stone," p. 62.

53 Waite, Arthur Edward. *The Real History of the Rosicrucians*, George Redway, London, 1887, p. 64.

54 *Ibid.*, p. 71.

55 *Ibid.*, p. 86.

56 *Ibid.*, p. 85.

57 *Ibid.*, p. 90.

58 Yates, Frances Amelia. *The Rosicrucian Enlightenment*, Routledge & Kegan Paul Ltd., London, pp. 48–49.

59 *Ibid.*, p. 31.

60 *Ibid.*, p. 207.

61 *Ibid.*, p. 91.

62 *Ibid.*, p. 211.

63 *Ibid.*

64 Minogue. *Out There Radio.*

65 Waite. *The Real History of the Rosicrucians*, p. 73.

66 Carlson. Unpublished interview.

67 Yates. *The Rosicrucian Enlightenment*, p. 87.

68 Carlson. Unpublished interview.

69 Osinski. "Mr. Christian, come here!"

CHAPTER 4: THE NEW WORLD ORDER

70 NsaneSk8er007. "A Message to the NWO from The Georgia Guidestones," YouTube, December 15, 2008. http://www.youtube.com/watch?v=pHw2WE9SCeo.

71 Google, Inc. has announced plans to shutter the Google Video service. At the time of writing the links to Google Video were live; if the service is terminated the video clips may be transferred to YouTube.

72 Author unknown. "Conversation with Sociopath Jim Stachowiak," Google Video, 2008. http://video.google.com/videoplay?docid=-4732688545396474765&hl=en&emb=1#

73 Aphrodite, Christie. "Georgia Guidestones Vandalized by 'Anonymous Patriot'?" Google Video, 2008. http://video.google.com/videoplay?docid=-3194999744154780966#

74 Stachowiak, Jim. *Freedom Fighter Radio*, "About," 2009. http://freedomfighterradio.net/about-site.

75 Stachowiak, Jim. "We Are Change and their Anti-2nd amendment Socialist/Communist connections X-posed," *Freedom Fighter Radio*, September 5, 2009. http://freedomfighterradio.net/2009/09/05/we-are-change-and-their-anti-2nd-amendment-sociolistcommunist-connections.

76 Stachowiak, Jim. "News and events that threaten our Freedom which the mainstream media avoids," *Freedom Fighter Radio*, TalkShoe.com, November 17, 2008, http://www.talkshoe.com/talkshoe/web/talkCast.jsp?masterId=18976&pageNumber=32&pageSize=15.

77 Aphrodite, Christie. *JimStachowiak.com*, "Home." http://www.jimstachowiak.com/index.php.

78 Unknown Author. "Jim Stachowiak FIRED from We Are Change for abusive psychotic behavior!" Google Video, 2008. http://video.google.com/videoplay?docid=-7009974409626230376#.

79 Stachowiak, Jim. "We Are Change and their Anti-2nd amendment Socialist/Communist connections X-posed," *Freedom Fighter Radio*,

September 5, 2009. http://freedomfighterradio.net/2009/09/05/we-are-change-and-their-anti-2nd-amendment-sociolistcommunist-connections.

80 JohnWdoe. "All parties in contact with Jim Stachowiak or freedomfighterradio.net should read this *important*" *Above Top Secret*, January 5, 2009. http://www.abovetopsecret.com/forum/thread459864/pg1.

81 Johnson, Eric. "Union Down," *Metro Spirit: Augusta's Independent Voice*, Issue 20.30. Portico Publications, February 18, 2009. http://metrospirit.com/index.php?cat=1993101074458954&ShowArticle_ID=11011702093391851.

82 *Ibid.*

83 *Endgame: Blueprint for Global Enslavement*. Dir. Alex Jones. Disinformation Company, 2007. DVD

84 Nichols, Lee. "Psst, It's a Conspiracy: KJFK Gives Alex Jones the Boot," *The Austin Chronicle*, Austin Chronicle Corp, December 10, 1999, http://www.austinchronicle.com/news/1999-12-10/75039.

85 *America: Wake Up (or Waco)*. Dir. Alex Jones. Infowars.com. Streaming Internet video.

86 *Ibid.*

87 *Ibid.*

88 *Endgame*, Dir. Jones.

89 *Ibid.*

90 *Ibid.*

91 *Ibid.*

92 *Ibid.*

93 *Ibid.*

94 *Dark Secrets Inside Bohemian Grove*. Dir. Alex Jones. PrisonPlanet.tv, 2000. Streaming Internet video.

95 *Ibid.*

96 *Ibid.*

97 *Ibid.*

98 *Ibid.*

99 *Secret Rulers of the World.* "Part 4: The Satanic Shadowy Elite?" Dir. Jon Ronson. World of Wonder Productions, 2001.

100 Ronson, Jon. *Them: Adventures with Extremists*, Simon and Schuster, 2002, p. 321.

101 "Mark Dice on the Alex Jones Show," Google Video, July 2005. http://video.google.com/videoplay?docid=2652622080193816045&hl=en#.

102 *Ibid.*

103 "'Lost It' Calls," *Coast to Coast AM*, December 1, 2006. Premiere Radio Networks.

104 "Mark Dice on the Alex Jones Show," Google Video.

105 "Is Jessica Simpson too gorgeous?" *The Daily Times*, July 8, 2005. http://www.dailytimes.com.pk/default.asp?page=story_8-7-2005_pg9_9.

106 Dice, Mark. *The Resistance Manifesto (Revised Edition)*. The Resistance, San Diego, CA, 2008, p. 309.

107 *Ibid.*

108 "Christians demand removal of 'satanic' 10 commandments." *World Net Daily*. July 28, 2008. WordNetDaily.com Inc. http://www.wnd.com/index.php?fa=PAGE.view&pageId=70792

109 "'Lost It' Calls," *Coast to Coast AM.*

110 *Ibid.*

111 Dice. *The Resistance Manifesto*, p. 315.

112 *Ibid.*

113 "'Lost It' Calls," *Coast to Coast AM.*

114 *Ibid.*

115 Dice. *The Resistance Manifesto*, p. 315.

116 *Ibid.*

117 "'Lost It' Calls," *Coast to Coast AM.*

118 *Ibid.*

119 *Ibid.*

120 Dice. *The Resistance Manifesto*, p. 315.

121 "Mark Dice on the Alex Jones Show," Google Video.

122 *Ibid.*

123 Dice. *The Resistance Manifesto*, p. 315.

124 *Ibid.*

125 *Ibid.*

126 Smith, Van. "A few words about last night's 'Brad Meltzer's Decoded'," *Van's Hardware Journal*, February 4, 2011. http://vanshardware.com/2011/02/a-few-words-about-tonights-brad-meltzers-decoded.

127 Smith, Van. "A Georgia Guidestones Update," *Van's Hardware Journal*, February 3, 2011. http://vanshardware.com/2011/02/a-georgia-guidestones-update.

128 *Ibid.*

129 "The Omega Hour: Van Smith – Georgia Guidestones," *Blog Talk Radio*, April 2, 2010. http://www.blogtalkradio.com/ministerfortson/2010/04/02/the-omega-hour-van-smith--georgia-guidestones.

130 Smith. "A Georgia Guidestones Update."

131 Smith, Van. "More Linkage between the Georgia Guidestones and the Burj Khalifa," *Van's Hardware Journal*, January 12, 2010. http://www.vanshardware.com/2010/01/more-linkage-between-georgia.html.

132 "The Omega Hour: Van Smith – Georgia Guidestones," *Blog Talk Radio*.

133 Smith. "A Georgia Guidestones Update."

134 *Ibid.*

135 *Ibid.*

136 *Ibid.*

137 Smith, Van. "Decoding the Georgia Guidestones." *Van's Hardware Journal*. December 28, 2009. http://www.vanshardware.com/2009/12/decoding-georgia-guidestone.html.

138 Smith. "A Georgia Guidestones Update."

139 Smith, Van. "Is this the face of R. C. Christian?" *Van's Hardware Journal*, March 17, 2010. http://vanshardware.com/2010/03/is-this-the-face-of-r-c-christian.

140 Smith. "A Georgia Guidestones Update."

141 *Ibid.*

142 Smith. "Decoding the Georgia Guidestones."

CHAPTER 5: THE MAN BEHIND THE MONUMENT

143 Christian. *Common Sense Renewed*, p. 7.

144 Elberton Granite Finishing Co., Inc. "The Georgia Guidestones," p. 5.

145 Martin. *The Guidestones*.

146 Sullivan. "American Stonehenge," p. 3.

147 Christian. *Common Sense Renewed*, p. 2.

148 Lewis. "Mystery in Stone," p. 59.

149 Christian. *Common Sense Renewed*. p. 7.

150 Smith, Matt. "Waiting for the end of the world: Georgia's 30-year stone mystery," *CNN*, March 22, 2010. http://www.cnn.com/2010/US/03/22/georgia.mystery.monument/?hpt=C2.

151 Martin. *The Guidestones*.

152 Sullivan. "American Stonehenge," p. 3.

153 Martin. *The Guidestones*.

154 James, Henry. "Wells and Salisbury," *Transatlantic Sketches*, University Press: Welch, Bigelow & Co. Cambridge. 1875, p. 54.

155 Elberton Granite Finishing Co., Inc. "The Georgia Guidestones," p. 38.

156 Christian. *Common Sense Renewe*, p. 89.

157 *Ibid.*, p. 88.

158 *Ibid.*, p. 94.

159 *Ibid.*, p. 87.

160 *Ibid.*, p. 88.

161 *Ibid.*, p. 89.

162 *Ibid.*, p. 86.

163 *Ibid.*, p. 7.

164 Paine, Thomas. *The Age of Reason*. G.N. Devries, New York, 1827, p. 5.

165 Christian. *Common Sense Renewed*, p. 94.

166 Paine. *The Age of Reason*, p. 13.

167 *Ibid.*, p. 3.

168 Christian. *Common Sense Renewed*, p. 4.

169 *Ibid.*, p. 46.

170 *Ibid.*, p. 58.

171 *Ibid.*, p. 59.

172 *Ibid.*, p. 46.

173 *Ibid.*, p. 43.

174 *Ibid.*, p. 39.

175 *Ibid.*, p. 58.

176 *Ibid.*, p. 41.

177 *Ibid.*, p. 64.

CHAPTER 6: ALTERNATIVES TO ARMAGEDDON

178 Radiation Effects Research Foundation. "Frequently Asked Questions." http://www.rerf.or.jp/general/qa_e/qa1.html.

179 Khrushchev, Nikita. As quoted in: *Time Magazine*. "Foreign News: We will bury you!" November 26, 1956.

180 Natural Resources Defense Council. "Table of Global Nuclear Weapons Stockpiles, 1945–2002," *Archive of Nuclear Data*. http://www.nrdc.org/nuclear/nudb/datab19.asp.

181 Christian. *Common Sense Renewed*, p. 7.

182 Elberton Granite Finishing Co., Inc. "The Georgia Guidestones," p. 11.

183 Christian. *Common Sense Renewed*, p. 3.

184 *Ibid.*, p. 71.

185 *Ibid.*, p. 126.

186 *Ibid.*, p. 35.

187 *Ibid.*, p. 110.

188 *Ibid.*, p. 71.

189 Martin. *The Guidestones*.

AFTERWORD

190 "The Fall and Rise of Dutchy, Elberton's First Granite Monument," The Elberton Granite Association. Elberton, Georgia, p. 3.

191 *Ibid*, p. 2.

192 *Ibid*.

193 *Ibid*.

194 Wimsatt Jr., W.K. and Monroe C. Beardsley. "The Intentional Fallacy," *The Verbal Icon: Studies of Meaning in Poetry*, University of Kentucky Press. Lexington, Kentucky. 1954, p. 3.

195 "The Fall and Rise of Dutchy." The Elberton Granite Association. p. 3.

196 Austin Gandy. *Out There Radio*.

www.guidestones.us

www.disinfo.com